Tips and Traps
When Buying
a Franchise

Tips and Traps When Buying a Franchise

Mary E. Tomzack

McGraw-Hill, Inc.

New York   San Francisco   Washington, D.C.   Auckland   Bogotá
Caracas   Lisbon   London   Madrid   Mexico City   Milan
Montreal   New Delhi   San Juan   Singapore
Sydney   Tokyo   Toronto

Library of Congress Cataloging-in-Publication Data

Tomzack, Mary E.
    Tips and traps when buying a franchise / by Mary E. Tomzack.
        p.   cm.
    Includes index.
    ISBN 0-07-065100-0 (HC)—ISBN 0-07-065101-9 (PBK)
    1. Franchises (Retail trade)—Management. 2. Small business—
Purchasing. I. Title.
HF5429.23.T66   1994
658.8'708—dc20   93-50118
                                                   CIP

 This book is printed on recycled, acid-free paper containing a minimum of 50% recycled de-inked fiber.

1 2 3 4 5 6 7 8 9 0 DOC/DOC 9 0 9 8 7 6 5 4

ISBN 0-07-065100-0 (HC)
ISBN 0-07-065101-9 (PBK)

The sponsoring editor for this book was David Conti, the editing supervisor was Jim Halston, and the production supervisor was Donald F. Schmidt. It was set in Baskerville by Carol Woolverton Studio in cooperation with Warren Publishing Services.

*To my two mentors
my father, Edward R. Tomzack,
and my husband, Michel Goldschneider*

Contents

Preface

Perhaps you are a casualty of big business downsizing and have decided that you'd like to strike out on a business of your own. Or maybe you're a woman or a member of an ethnic or racial minority and you're looking for the so-called "level playing field." Then again you may already be in business for yourself but not achieving the results you want. For all of you, and others who simply want a chance at running your own business, a franchise business may be the solution.

According to a recent Arthur Anderson study commissioned by the International Franchising Association, franchising is running counter to current United States slow-to-no growth patterns, with a growth rate of nearly 15% for 1992. In general this growth can be attributed to several factors: the number of corporate workers seeking new avenues, the rising appeal of entrepreneurship, and changing consumer needs.

The same study also reports that 96.9% of the franchised units opened in the last 5 years are still in operation today. As we read further, we find, however, a more important figure cited—85.7% are still operated by the original franchise owner. The difference between the two figures leaves 9–10% who, I suspect, did not give up their franchises in the face of success. Perhaps their unsuccessful units were repurchased by the franchisor which, in turn, resold them or took over their operations. In these cases, the franchise system would call them buyouts or terminations of the agreement, but not failures. The goal of this book is to steer you towards success and away from failure, so that in five years you will be part of the 85.7%.

What I Learned

In the course of research for this book I interviewed more than 50 franchisees in a variety of businesses across the United States and many industry experts. I especially stayed away from lengthy conversations with franchisors, preferring to see the whole process through the franchisee's eyes. The interviews revealed many interesting insights "from those in the trenches" which I will share with you throughout the book. A selection of statistics derived from the 50 plus franchisee interviews is in Chapter 11.

But there is one overriding principle, which all the research and interviews bore out, and that is—Making the *Right* Initial Choice of Franchise Is 95% of the Success Recipe. Of course, hard work and a good business sense are also necessary, but for the readers of this book we will take that as a given. I am convinced that if you read this book carefully and take the time to do the necessary investigations and analysis your chances of success as a franchisee are assured.

Mary E. Tomzack

Acknowledgments

In order to write this book, I called on the expertise of several people who unstintingly shared information, insights, and advice with me. In particular, I am grateful for the help of the following and send them many thanks.

Bret Lowell, Esq.

Terrian Barnes-Bryant, IFA

Nancy L. Minter, IFA

Bob Jones, IFA

Dan Lasman, Hampstead Partners

Richard A. Clapsaddle, CPA

Carl Carlsson, Franchise Business USA

and

a special thanks to the editor of this book, Caroline Carney

and

for their enthusiasm and support, thanks to my mother, Mary R. Tomzack, and my children, Vanessa and Evan Goldschneider.

The franchisees I interviewed for this book were gracious in giving so freely of their time—even with their hectic schedules—and willingly shared their past experiences. They made a special effort to tell me what they had learned in their franchise businesses so that I could transmit ideas and advice to you, the prospective franchisee. I want to thank them for their help. They are:

Kitty Alaily, Cost Cutters, City Looks, Wisconsin

Fred Banty, Padgett Business Services, Connecticut

Steven Bashein, Alphagraphics, Washington, D.C.

Ann Brown, Computertots, Washington, D.C. and Maryland

Lisa Brumm, Formals Etc., Illinois

Mike Bueti, Merry Maids, New York

Ray Chappell and Paula Ford, Dent Doctor, Texas

George Colgate, VR Business Brokers, Tennessee

Carla Cunningham, Jani-King, Pennsylvania

Mary Cunningham, Decorating Den, Maryland

Camille DiNapoli, Subway, New York

Ken Dykhuis, Mighty Distributing Co., Illinois

Jeanette Fuller, Tutor Time, Florida

Larry Gambino, Priority Management Co., New York

Judy Gedman, FastSigns, New Mexico

Jim Gendreau, Cost Cutters, Minnesota

Leslie Goldberg, Expressions Custom Furniture, New York

Jeff Grayson, Pizzeria Uno, Florida

Arny Greshkin, Unishippers, Connecticut

Rich Habel, Mail Boxes, Etc., Washington, D.C.

Florence and George Hayden, Wendy's, Pennsylvania

Jeff Knight, GNC, New York

Danny Kostick, Pizza Hut, Pennsylvania

George Lawson, Red Hot & Blue, South Carolina

Nancy Mann, Citizens Against Crime, Georgia

Joan Maruyama, A Choice Nanny, Virginia

Robert Marziano, Aloette Cosmetics, New Jersey

Patrick McClune, Pressed 4 Time, New Jersey

Jay McDuffie, Check Express, Alabama

Linda Moore, Ledger Plus, Massachusetts

Eleanor Nesbit, A Choice Nanny, Florida

Tom Orban, I Can't Believe It's Yogurt, Pennsylvania, Virginia, Washington, D.C., Maryland

Barry Pasarew, Voice-tel, Texas

Rick Petersen, Interim Healthcare, New Hampshire

Carolyn Peterson, Headshots, New York

Marcy Pinnell, Wee-bag-it, Missouri

Barry Roberts, Execu-Train, New Jersey

Stuart and Sharon Ruben, Money Mailer, Connecticut and New York

Lisa Rutledge, Kinderdance Intl., North Carolina

Steve Saffar, The Wedding Pages, New Jersey and New York

Harold Sanchez, GNC, Connecticut

Glenn and Connie Schenenga, Future Kids, New York

Tom Swarm, Motophoto, Washington, D.C. and Maryland

Sharon Taylor, Potions & Lotions, New Mexico

Grace Thompson, Leadership Management Inc., Pennsylvania

Sandi Vettle, Leadership Management Inc., Pennsylvania

Ken Wisotsky, Gloria Jean's Coffee Bean, My Favorite Muffin, New Jersey

and about a half dozen franchisees who prefer to remain anonymous.

1

Franchising
for the 90s

Many industry experts believe that the 1990s will be the best decade in history for franchising. To be sure, a confluence of events and conditions make this prediction a pretty sure bet:

- The increasing number of highly qualified prospective franchisees, the "new franchisees"
- The lowest interest rates since 1963
- Greater availability of prime locations due to real estate failures
- More favorable leases in most parts of the country because of the weak economy of the last few years
- A greater diversity of ownership as franchisors use attractive financing and special deals to recruit women, minorities, and veterans

Not only will the 90s be a period of phenomenal growth for franchising, but the perception of this business concept may be changing as well. If you think of a franchise business as a small, limited, Mom-and-Pop-type operation, you may be in for some surprises. Franchising in the 90s will, of course, still consist of single-unit franchisees but, increasingly, the new franchisee will be a multiunit owner or a developer of a large region or territory. The franchisee of the 90s is very likely to be the owner and manager of a sizeable corporate entity. And, incidentally, most franchise systems are encouraging this trend.

Franchising Formats

Unless you've been living on another planet, you probably are already somewhat familiar with franchising. You may even patronize a variety of franchise businesses without realizing that they are franchises. The businesses run the gamut from car servicing and financial services to yogurt and voice mail. With franchise businesses responsible for about one-third of all retail sales in the United States and a predicted 50 percent of all sales by the year 2000, franchises are difficult to escape.

However, you may not know that there are two types of franchises: product and trade name franchises and business format franchises. In the former, the franchisee has use of a product or trade name but no supporting relationship with the franchisor. This means that the franchisee basically operates the business independently but does benefit from the marketing and advertising efforts of the franchise system. The products which are franchised are generally the older, established ones with a proven customer base. Product and trade name franchises are most commonly auto dealerships, gas stations, and soft-drink bottling companies. The business format franchise is faster growing and is the format we will discuss in this book. It is characterized by an ongoing business relationship between franchisor and franchisee. The franchisee is offered not only a trademark and logo but also a complete system of doing business. Business format franchises are famous throughout the world with participants such as McDonald's, Holiday Inn, Midas, Century 21, and Baskin-Robbins, to name a few.

In the best of all worlds, the business format franchise is mutually beneficial, for franchisor and franchisee alike. The franchisee, by paying an initial fee and, often, an ongoing royalty, gives the franchise system a continuous supply of working capital to develop and expand the organization. In turn, the franchisee gets a business package which would take years to develop and refine, a strengthened ability to compete through the established brand identity and marketing power of the system, and the cost benefits and clout of the franchisor's collective purchasing power.

"Buying" a Franchise

Now that you're excited about franchise opportunities, I'm going to tell you something that may disappoint you: You cannot "buy" a franchise. In actuality you are engaging in a "leasing" transaction. Why is it a lease? In any franchise deal the franchisee receives the assets upfront but only for a period of time—the term of the franchise agreement. The term of the agreement may run 5 or 10 years or, in some cases, only 1 or 2. Renewals of these agreements are at the option of the franchisor, and the reasons for not renewing an agreement should be completely spelled out in the Uniform Franchise Offering Circular (UFOC) and franchise agreement (see Chapter 5).

The fact that you are leasing and not purchasing a franchise may not influence your decision to become a franchisee, but this distinction must be kept in mind during the analytical, negotiating, and agreement processes.

There are other important considerations as well. First, you must determine if you would function well as a franchisee. If so, you then have to choose the right franchise among the 3000-plus franchise selections available. That's only the beginning. After you whittle your franchise choices down to, maybe, a half dozen, you must then thoroughly investigate each opportunity. Once the choice is made, your job is to analyze and understand the franchise agreement and, if possible, negotiate points of disagreement with the franchisor. Finally, you will have to put together a financial package to fund your franchise investment. The rest of this book is dedicated to exploring these issues and giving you the facts and practical knowledge that will result in a satisfying franchise selection.

2

What Makes a Good Franchisee?

A good candidate for a franchise is a person who worked hard at a previous position. Someone who is "dead-wood" in a job will fail at a franchise.

LARRY GAMBINO
Priority Management franchisee

The average franchise owner, according to the January 1993 issue of *Entrepreneur* magazine, is 40 years old and has a net worth of $329,704. Ninety percent of the franchisees are college-educated, 20 percent are women, 11 percent are minorities, and more than one-third are "corporate refugees." The magazine also finds that today's franchisees have more business savvy and greater expectations. Unlike 20 years ago, the new franchisee is apt to be a corporate dropout, a woman, or a minority.

In fact, even the motivation for owning a franchise has changed in the last few years. Previously, the most common reasons for opening a franchise were a desire to be your own boss, a dream of financial growth and riches, a need to work with an experienced company and get a "head start," and a perception that the franchised business would be an asset of lasting value. Today the motivation to buy a franchise goes beyond personal objectives to include extenuating circumstances. These reasons (from our survey) are the most common:

- The massive restructuring in the corporate sector that eliminated jobs, forced industries to relocate, and encouraged employees to take an early retirement
- Discouragement with the U.S. corporate environment and its slack promotions, lack of appreciation, and more work for less pay
- Career change (tired of old job, burnout)
- A dream of owning own business
- Changing from an independent business owner to a franchisee
- Previous experience in a franchise system
- Franchise considered a good business opportunity
- Desire for independence
- Second career for early retiree

The Qualifying Process

The majority of franchise systems will do a thorough background check of a potential franchisee. The typical screening process will analyze an applicant's resources, experience, and character. (See the sample qualifying questionnaire at the end of this chapter.)

Most likely, the first qualification considered and the very first thing investigated is the prospect's financial situation. A qualifying questionnaire will include the following information:

Assets—include cash, home market value, savings funds, other real estate, stocks, bonds, and securities, insurance (cash value), automobile, your own business, notes receivable, other assets

Liabilities—include loans and notes payable, charge accounts, real estate mortgages, loans against life insurance, other indebtedness

Net worth—total assets less total liabilities

Sources of income—include salary, bonus and commissions, dividends and interest, real estate income, other sources

This same qualifying questionnaire will ask questions about your educational history and previous employment. Often you are asked to supply names of credit references and personal references.

Many franchisors also ask questions to determine the candidate's motivation to buy a franchise and to find out more about his or her personal characteristics. You may expect questions such as: Why are you interested in becoming associated with XYZ franchise? Why do you think you would be successful in XYZ franchise? What are your goals for the next 3 years?

If you "pass" the first questionnaire and are asked to come to the corporate or regional headquarters for further discussion, you can expect additional questions of this kind and may even be given a type of personality quiz to see if you have the right temperament to run the franchise successfully.

Tip

On your first visit to corporate headquarters, you're not the only one being appraised. This is the time for you to evaluate the franchise management, both in style and in substance.

The Ideal Franchisee

Do you have the necessary qualities to succeed as a franchisee? Answering this question entails a great deal of the proverbial "soul searching." Ask yourself if you have a strong desire for achievement. This is a common trait for success in both a franchise and an independent business.

Here is a checklist of questions which will get you on the right track for your self-analysis.

1. *Are you able to work within the structure of a franchise system?* With a franchise you'll be buying into a proven business system with proscribed ways of operating. Many of the decisions have already been

made for you. If you need to control everything or like to make all the decisions yourself, this could pose a problem.

2. *Are you "buying a job"?* Think carefully about your reasons for considering a franchise. If you have been unemployed or underemployed for some time, operating a franchise can seem an enticing solution. Self-employment is not for everyone and certainly is not a panacea for joblessness.

3. *Are you prepared to work long hours to make the business succeed?* There's just no getting around it. Even with the assistance of the franchisor staff, there will not be enough hours in the day to do everything. The first few years will be especially stressful.

4. *Are you able to work without supervision and a support staff?* Although you will have the structure of the franchise system, the day-to-day decisions will have to be made in a timely fashion. In all likelihood you won't be getting input from any employees, so you will have to make the decisions alone. In addition, you'll probably have the job of choosing and placing advertising materials as well as running the copier machine. You'll have to wear many hats.

5. *Are you mentally prepared for financial risk?* You'll be signing documents with investors and lending institutions and maybe leasing companies and others. Although you will try to minimize your business risk by choosing wisely, financial risk is always present.

6. *Is your spouse supportive of you starting a business?* Whether the spouse works in the business or not, 100 percent support is a necessity if you want both the business and the marriage to continue.

7. *Are you able to organize your time?* Since time is your most precious commodity you must be able to strip away the nonessentials and prioritize the rest.

8. *Do you give up easily if things don't go as well as planned?* Any new business will have its peaks and valleys. You will have to be persistent about reaching your goals and look at momentary setbacks as just part of the process.

Tip

Don't be upset if the result of your self-appraisal is not positive for franchising. After all, the objective of the analysis is not to buy a franchise but to avoid making a mistake.

From the Franchisor's Viewpoint

To be sure, the ideal franchisee is rare, but most franchisors look for the following characteristics in their franchisees:

- A person with a strong motivation and drive to achieve success
- A person with confidence and enthusiasm for the product or service being sold, rather than just a desire to make a profit
- A person who does *not* have all the administrative and entrepreneurial skills necessary to start, develop, and operate a viable business and who therefore needs the franchisor's support (a front-line supervisor or middle manager would be a good choice rather than someone who is a self-starter and has already founded a business)
- A person who not only is good at learning new things but who also is able to motivate and train others
- A person with at least 5 years of managerial or teaching experience
- A person who has experience in or a good knowledge of the industry in which the franchisor does business

A few industries, most notably some fast-food systems, do not seek the last qualification. Several fast-food systems automatically disqualify applicants with a restaurant background. The idea here is that a franchisee freshly trained in the franchisor's procedures will be more successful than one coming in from the same industry with different and often conflicting habits.

Likewise, many hair and beauty salon franchises will not recruit technical people (such as hair stylists and cosmetologists). Instead they look to business people with no hair styling or beauty skills to become franchisees. The franchisors believe that management skills, attention to customer service, and sales skills are the most important qualifications.

Tip

In order to qualify, some systems, such as McDonald's and Domino's, require that the prospective franchisee works as an employee in a pilot program before buying the franchise. Though time consuming and arduous, this technique nearly eliminates the risk of failure as a franchisee.

From the Franchisee Viewpoint

When I asked franchisees "What makes a good franchisee?" they gave one overwhelming answer—*a good salesperson.* Just about every franchisee—from businesses as diverse as management training to high-tech printing to residential cleaning to check cashing—mentioned sales skills as a prime requisite. Quite a few people also expressed surprise at the amount of time taken up by the sales and marketing duties. Those franchisees who had no experience in sales were at a distinct disadvantage and had to learn in a hurry or else lose the business.

Tip

If you have no experience with sales and don't care to learn, better think twice about buying a franchise.

As an offshoot of the emphasis on sales in all the businesses, franchisees mentioned that you need a healthy self-image to handle all the rejections that will certainly come your way. You can't be a "fragile " person, one franchisee's terminology for someone who will take every rejection as a personal affront. The most successful franchisees look at the sales function as a numbers game where if they persist in their efforts they will reach their goals.

On a par with a sales orientation, the other quality necessary for a franchisee is a high energy level. Almost all the franchisees talk about the long hours, maybe 80 hours a week in some cases. The bigger frustration, however, is not receiving a salary which is commensurate with the amount of time and effort. A franchisee can expect a slim salary for a tremendous amount of work, at least for the first year or two of operating the business. So in addition to a high energy level a certain resiliency is also necessary.

Should You Start Your Own?

A recent U.S. Department of Commerce study shows that 97 percent of franchise businesses are still operating after the first year—as compared to 62 percent of the independent small businesses. The contrast becomes even more dramatic after five years when 92 percent of franchised businesses are still operating as compared to 23 percent of independent businesses.

This sounds like an impressive case for franchises. Let's take a closer look at the choice of operating an independent or a franchise business. In our own survey of franchisees, 12 percent had been independent business people before buying into a franchise. The switch from independent to franchisee appears to be something of a minitrend. Some of the reasons for switching include better name recognition, superior sales and marketing materials, and access to cost-effective suppliers and better locations.

When it comes to making your own decision between opening an independent business or buying into a franchise system, the statistics can tell you only so much. To make the right decision, you'll have to take stock of your personality, working style, access to financing, and risk sensitivity.

Interestingly enough, the majority of both franchisees and independent business people share one quality. They value independence over security. Where they differ most is their risk threshold and their tolerance for bureaucracy. The true entrepreneur will be willing to live with risk (sometimes extreme) if the projected payoff is sufficient and will have a very low tolerance for controls and procedures. The "ideal franchisee," however, is somewhat risk-adverse and is willing to pay the price (the franchise fee and royalties) to diminish the overall risk of failure. This franchisee will also faithfully follow controls and procedures. After all, the system is part of the purchase price, and strict adherence to its tenets promises success.

The entrepreneur—the type most likely to succeed as an independent businessperson—will sometimes find her or his application rejected by the franchisor. Since conformity to the franchisor's format and operating dictums are critical for success, the franchisor will reject anyone who seems to show resistance to standard operating procedures. Franchisors also believe that entrepreneurs may be openly critical of things they don't like, may lose interest in the routine tasks of running the franchise, and may quickly start to look for the next challenge.

Tip

Don't count yourself out if you have a true entrepreneurial personality. Large area developing, multiunit franchising, and international franchising can be perfect for the entrepreneur. These franchise formats provide constant new challenges and a degree of control almost equal to that of the franchisor.

Franchisees Who Have Been There

Most of the franchisees in our survey had to make a decision first on whether they would open an independent business or a franchised one. A few of their stories follow.

Before a New Jersey man decided to buy a food franchise business, he asked himself this question: "How comfortable do I feel about going into the unknown?" He answered, "Not very." Although he was familiar with engineering work, manufacturing, and construction, he knew very little about the food business. Even so, he purchased a snack foods business. Now after nearly 10 years of operation, he is ready to give up on the franchise. His goal is to open and operate five independent stores that carry similar products. Not only has the ownership of the franchise system changed several times, but he believes that "the franchise system squashes the creativeness of the individual. You can be prohibited from bringing anything new into the system."

Barry Pasarew is a Voice-Tel franchisee in the high-tech voice message business. The business utilizes sophisticated equipment and elaborate service networks. Pasarew says, "It would be close to impossible to do this business on your own because of the necessity of a network. The franchise system allows you to get started immediately. It saves dollars and time so you can focus on selling and developing."

Jim Gendreau owns an independent distribution company but was still drawn to franchises. He owns multiunits of the Cost Cutters franchise which is in the hair salon business. When asked why he didn't start the business independently, especially since he was an experienced businessperson, he said, "The big difference between an independent and a franchise is the marketing and advertising clout and expertise the franchise brings. Secondly, all the bugs are out of the system by the time you buy it."

Linda Moore, a Ledger Plus franchisee, considered both an independent and a franchise business after leaving a position in a large corporation. She says, "Unless you have a very unique business idea, it's almost foolish not to buy a franchise. Success rates are not as good for independents. Most people have skills in one or two areas, and with a franchise you can get help in areas outside your expertise."

Ken Wisotzky had an independent ice cream store previous to owning two franchises, Gloria Jean's and My Favorite Muffin. The ice cream business was going well, so why didn't he continue? Wisotzky says, "The mall developer wouldn't renew the lease on my store. They wanted a 'name brand' tenant." He believes that many developers, realtors, and landlords consider franchises stronger tenants, and so the franchisee can get better space.

When faced with making a decision on buying a mobile laundry and dry-cleaning franchise, Patrick McClune's wife and friends advised him to "do it himself." They told him, "You're smart and resourceful and you shouldn't pay for a logo that's not very well known." McClune asked the franchise system what he was getting that was proprietary. They said that he would receive training, the system for doing business, and the logo. So, McClune went with the franchise and now concludes that the franchise did give him a "jumpstart" and a good system for conducting business.

Tip

Sometimes the choice between independent and franchise depends on the type of business. A publishing business franchisee told me, "Fast food, for example, needs a name company. A franchise works best. Publishing, on the other hand, is a business you may be able to do independently. For example, I have a competitor which is an independent business, and it does at least as well as we do."

The New Pool

Ex-corporate workers, women, minorities, retired military—do they have potential as franchisees? Do they have the general qualities necessary for success? On the whole, franchising is a good match with the skills, ambitions, experiences, and needs of many people in these groups.

The Corporate Dropout

The corporate dropout has several advantages. Many corporate workers are used to *systems,* and this is exactly what you're buying with a franchise, so immediately these workers feel a degree of comfort and familiarity. Their expertise and experience are also often transferable to a franchise. For example, many have experience in sales and marketing which is a real asset for almost all types of franchises. If they were line managers, they have a financial background which is invaluable in businesses where cash flow is critical. Then, too, they tend to be computer literate, which gives them an edge using the software programs the franchisor provides for administrative and accounting purposes. All these skills can help the ex-corporate worker get off to a faster start than the average franchisee.

An illustration of this corporate experience edge can be seen in a Mail Boxes, Etc. franchise in Washington, D.C. Rich Habel, the franchisee, had previously worked for a major corporation where his self-discipline and customer service skills helped him to succeed. He's found these abilities equally important and applicable to his shipping business.

In some instances, though, corporate experience can work against you. For example, some franchise systems don't look upon ex-corporate workers as ideal candidates. Although no franchisewide figures are available, it is rumored that some systems reject 25 to 30 percent of the ex-corporate worker applicants. Some of the reasons given for rejection are:

- Ex-corporate workers are not used to functioning without a support staff. Unlike the corporate world, the boss must wear a lot of hats because there are fewer employees.
- They do not pay attention to bottom line figures and lack a profit orientation. Often previous corporate experience simply dictates that the person operate "within the budget."
- They are not psychologically suited to the rough-and-tumble world of franchising after the somewhat sheltered and structured corporate environment.

- They lack entrepreneurial spirit. They need not only a willingness to follow the system, but also a high energy level and drive to excel.

Although few franchise systems will actually reject an enthusiastic and financially qualified ex-corporate worker, there is no doubt that some of these perceptions will surface in the first meeting with the franchisor. They are valid assessments of some ex-corporate people, and you need to think carefully about whether they apply to you. After all, the purpose of all the discussions and appraisals is to avoid making a mistake which can prove to be both financially and personally painful.

A great number of ex-corporate people, however, are succeeding very well in spite of some franchisor's apprehension. Fred Banty, a Padgett Business Service franchisee, has some ideas on why this works. He says, "For an ex-corporate person a franchise is like having a network and support around you (as in a corporation). It's not as scary or risky as an independent business. Franchises push you to market the product or service—give you a standard operating procedure—and will take up the slack for insufficient entrepreneurial skills."

Tip

Be Realistic and patient. Ex-corporate workers must realize that they will be going from a predictable weekly income to close to zero for the first year or more. Thereafter—maybe in several years—a viable income will follow. The saving grace: the *potential* for a large income is better at your own business than as a corporate employee.

An interesting trend is being observed in a number and variety of franchise systems. Although some of the personality traits and experiences of a corporate worker don't always lend themselves to a single-unit franchise, a multiunit franchise may work perfectly!

What accounts for this? It seems that as the franchisee acquires additional units, the job evolves from that of a worker/manager to that of a CEO. This is when organizational and communication skills come into play and when executive capabilities become an important ingredient in the success of the multiunit system.

If the slow and tedious pace of a corporate job is a major reason for you to leave, operating a franchise should be a good choice. If, however, you want to leave the corporation because of stress and long hours, don't buy a franchise. Most franchisees work 60 to 85 hours a week—at least in the beginning—and stress is often present.

Women

The U.S. Department of Commerce reports that women are opening businesses twice as fast as men, and many of these women are taking a look at franchises. Most of these prospective owners fall into one of two camps. Either they are corporate workers looking for a faster track in private enterprise, having hit the "glass ceiling," or they are complete novices who believe they can "buy" the necessary business acumen by signing on with a franchisor. They expect the franchisor to teach them how to operate and manage a profitable business.

Other women are drawn to franchising because of the flexibility and personal freedom of running their own business. In spite of all the hard work and long hours, owning a business often makes juggling home, children, and career a possibility.

Although women who are ex-corporate workers will have to confront negative perceptions some franchisors have, most franchisors believe women can be good franchisees, and, in fact, many are actively seeking women owners. For evidence of this, one need only look at the abundance of franchise advertisements in women's magazines.

When asked, many franchisors say women make good franchisees because they excel at team building and cooperative efforts, both of which are foundations of the franchise system. Franchisors also note that women seem to be more enthusiastic about the support and structure inherent in a franchise system. "Attention to detail" is also mentioned as a quality which is a real plus for women franchisees. For example, several of the women who own fast-food franchises showed their immaculate restrooms, an area that often falls by the wayside in this fast-paced industry. Not so for these owners who made cleanliness a top priority. The franchise systems, in their frequent unannounced inspections, notice the difference and give women owners/co-owners high marks.

The one big obstacle for women—although it's decreasing—is the difficulty in raising start-up capital. Traditionally, banks have been reluctant to lend money to women for new businesses (although men have not fared that well with banks either). In the few instances where a woman secures a bank loan for a new business, she will often be asked to have a cosigner—a husband or father. On the plus side, more and more franchise systems are offering financial help in one form or another, and a determined woman can probably find help there or tap into one of the special government programs.

Best Franchises for Women

Women are flocking to franchising in increasing numbers. In the random survey done for this book, 52 percent of the owners or co-owners were women. Many of the ones with corporate experience are opting for the business service franchises, such as leadership training, motivational seminars, accounting services, and the like.

Sandi Vettle and Grace Thompson, both from large corporations, are Leadership Management franchisees. When asked why they chose a franchise business, this is what they had to say. Vettle says, "I didn't want to have to reinvent the wheel. I also needed some good programming tools and especially the psychological support." Thompson's explanation is that "the quality of the materials [from the franchise] is so excellent and professionally done that it would be difficult to duplicate independently. The investment of time and energy to try and do it yourself just isn't worth it."

Some franchise systems, such as Decorating Den and A Choice Nanny sell nearly all their units to women. Other businesses traditionally attracting women are the retail, health and beauty, and cleaning services sectors. But more and more women are moving into less traditional areas. For example, women are seen in increasing numbers in businesses such as automotive services, security systems, and restaurants.

An Untraditional Franchisee

Paula Ford is a subfranchisee of Dent Doctor, a paintless dent removal business. Her brother-in-law, Ray Chappell, is the master franchisee for a large territory in Texas and Oklahoma, and Paula works a portion of the territory, paying a percentage of her sales to Ray as a subfranchisee (the company calls her an "associate").

Leaving a corporate secretarial position because she "was fed up with it," Paula admits that giving up a regular paycheck was a little scary for her. She considered looking for another job but found her job opportunities very limited. It was then that the idea of joining her brother-in-law in the dent removal business came to her.

After attending a bare minimum of training—three weeks at the corporate center, Paula continued with another five weeks of hands-on training with Ray. Even so, the work was so painstaking and difficult that, in the beginning, she was only able to work on small hail damage. She couldn't work very fast or on very big dents. Now, though, after only a year on the job, all that has changed, and her productivity has increased greatly.

Best of all, Paula finds that she is really happy with what she is doing. She loves the independence and making her own hours. Paula recalls, "The most negative thing about being a secretary was that if something went wrong it was your fault, whether you had control of it or not. On the other hand you didn't get recognition if things went well." Now Paula gets direct feedback from her customers, and she loves when they praise her for a good job.

How does the rest of the world look at a woman knocking out car dents? Paula says there has been little reaction from the customers—as long as she gets the job done. She admits that as a physically small woman, there are some larger dents she won't take on because of the sheer physical force needed to repair them.

As to whether she would make the same choice one year later, the answer is definitely yes. Since the business is almost all labor, with very little overhead, she started making a profit from the beginning. In fact, says Paula, "the first week out of training I made what it would have taken me a month to do in my previous job."

Minorities

About 10 percent of the franchises in the United States are operated by minorities, specifically, blacks, Hispanics, Asians, and native Americans. Terrian Barnes-Bryant, vice president of Research, Minority and Women's Affairs, at the International Franchise Association (IFA), says strong efforts are under way to increase minority participation. In fact, the IFA, the largest and oldest franchisor organization, is challenging its members to set up minority recruitment programs and expand minority career opportunities. To support this initiative, the IFA has also formed alliances with such groups as the NAACP, the U.S. Hispanic Chamber of Commerce, and the U.S. Commerce Department's Minority Business Development Agency.

Franchisors actively recruiting minorities usually want these franchisees to operate in inner cities and to deal with customers from a similar ethnic background. Fast-food operations and restaurants are the most active of the franchise businesses, with special programs for training and financing minority operations. Most notable are KFC Corporation, Hardee's, Shoney's, Captain D's Seafood, and Lee's Famous Recipe Country Chicken.

Retired Military

Across the board, franchisors are targeting ex-military personnel as potential franchisees. The pool of retired military is formidable and continues to grow. There are already almost 27 million veterans in the United States, and 350,000 more leave the armed services each year due to defense cuts.

Franchisors agree that experience with the military system translates to a healthy respect for and adherence to a franchise system's way of doing business. They find that military people respect the value of training, are enthusiastic learners, and follow orders. As an added plus, many ex-military are trained in sophisticated technological systems, enabling them to quickly learn computer systems and technologically based businesses.

Often the only obstacle for the prospective veteran franchisee is lack of capital. Most retirees do have pensions or retirement benefits which enable them to buy some of the low-investment franchises. However, the bulk of the franchises are beyond their financial means. Although this remains a problem, an organization called VETFRAN is doing its best to enlarge the choices open to veterans in franchising by signing up franchisors who will discount or finance their franchise fee for veterans.

Final Words

The first step in our exploration of franchise opportunities is a self-analysis. Think carefully about whether you have the necessary traits to succeed—traits such as a strong desire for achievement, a high energy level, persistence in reaching a goal, self-motivation, and a sales orientation. Be brutally honest in your appraisal and only continue the franchise search if your temperament and personality fit the bill.

PERSONAL DATA AND BUSINESS HISTORY:

NAME						AGE
HOME ADDRESS					NO. OF YEARS IN AREA	
CITY			STATE			ZIP
SOCIAL SECURITY			DATE OF BIRTH			
SPOUSE FIRST NAME			OCCUPATION			
NO. OF DEPENDENTS			AGES			

	AREA CODE	NUMBER		AREA	NUMBER
HOME PHONE			BUSINESS PHONE		

BUSINESS ADDRESS

OTHER BUSINESS CONNECTIONS (Officer, Director, Owner, Partner, etc.)

	FROM	TO	FIRM	POSITION	ANNUAL INCOME
BUSINESS EXPERIENCE					

Figure 2-1. Sample qualifying questionnaire.

PERSONAL DATA AND BUSINESS HISTORY - continued

EXACT NATURE OF BUSINESS EXPERIENCE (including self employment)
_____
_____
_____
_____
_____
_____
_____
_____

DO YOU NOW OWN ANY FRANCHISE? (describe)
_____

HAVE YOU EVER FAILED IN BUSINESS OR COMPROMISED WITH CREDITORS? IF YOU HAVE, WHEN, WHERE, CIRCUMSTANCES (including any remaining liabilities)
_____

ARE ANY LAWSUITS PENDING AGAINST YOU? (if yes — give particulars)
_____
HAVE YOU EVER BEEN CONVICTED OF A CRIME (except traffic misdemeanors)? If yes, give particulars.
_____

EDUCATION	DEGREE OR LEVEL ATTAINED	YEAR GRADUATED	MILITARY	Dates and Rank
1.				
2.				
3.				

HOW IS YOUR HEALTH?   U.S. CITIZEN?
WHAT PROFESSIONAL MAGAZINES AND TRADE JOURNALS DO YOUR READ?
DO YOU OWN ANY PATENTS OR COPYRIGHTS?
HOBBIES?

BUSINESS REFERENCES:

	INDIVIDUAL	TITLE	COMPANY	CITY	PHONE
1.					
2.					
3.					

CHARACTER REFERENCES:

1.		ADDRESS	PHONE
2.		ADDRESS	PHONE
3.		ADDRESS	PHONE

MEMBERSHIPS (Civic, business, professional):
_____
_____
_____

Figure 2-1. (*Continued*)

FINANCIAL DATA:

YOUR PERSONAL BANK _____ CONTACT _____

ADDRESS _____ CITY _____ PHONE _____

YOUR BUSINESS BANK _____ CONTACT _____

ADDRESS _____ CITY _____ PHONE _____

ASSETS	TOTAL
CASH	
SECURITIES - READILY NEGOTIABLE	
REAL ESTATE - FAIR MARKET VALUE, RESIDENCE	
REAL ESTATE - FAIR MARKET VALUE, OTHER	
NOTES RECEIVABLE	
BUSINESS VENTURES - LIQUID	
BUSINESS VENTURES - NON-LIQUID	
LIFE INSURANCE CASH VALUE	
RETIREMENT FUND	
INCOME TAX FUND	
ALL OTHER ASSETS	
TOTAL ASSETS	$

LIABILITIES	MONTHLY PAYMENT	TOTAL
MORTGAGES 1ST - RESIDENCE		
MORTGAGES 2ND - RESIDENCE		
MORTGAGES - OTHER		
LINES OF CREDIT		
VEHICLE/BOAT LOANS		
CREDIT CARD AND ALL OTHER LIABILITIES		
TOTAL LIABILITIES		$
NET WORTH		$

How do you propose to fund this investment?

_____

_____

_____

_____

Figure 2-1. (*Continued*)

MANAGEMENT PLANS:

If you were approved, when could you begin training? _____

Territory in which you are interested?   (1st Choice) _____
                                          (2nd Choice) _____

Are there any investor-associates who would join you in this venture? (Please have each fill out one of these forms.)
Names: _____
       _____
       _____
       _____

COMMENTS:

Please use this space to tell us anything else you think is relevant, i.e. your present business objectives, and as I consider my experiences and abilities, I am confident that I can operate a successful franchise primarily because:

_____
_____
_____
_____
_____
_____
_____
_____

To the best of my knowledge and ability the information I have submitted is correct.

_____   _____
Signature   Date

Figure 2-1. (Continued)

3

Choosing the Right Franchise

Enjoying what I'm doing is the prime
motivation, not money and not
independence. None of these is as
important as the pure enjoyment of liking
what you're doing.   **BARRY ROBERTS**
                        Executrain franchisee

In this chapter and the next I'm going to tell you how to *choose the right franchise*. Remember this is not an easy task with over 3000 franchise systems to choose from. But, however painstaking and time-consuming the process becomes, it's worth it! I am convinced that if you choose a franchise wisely your chances of success are almost assured.

Setting Priorities

If you remember one thing from this book, it should be this: before making any decision on a franchise, sit down, analyze your needs, capabilities, and limitations in relation to a franchise business. This could take as little as a few days or as much as several years. In either case, it is the most important step, so don't skip it.

Let's say you have looked at independent businesses and franchises and have definitely decided that a franchise business is for you. Your next step is to carefully answer questions like the following:

- Where will the business be located? In the city, the suburbs, the countryside? Do I want to commute? If so, what are the time limits? 30 minutes? 60 minutes?
- Do I want a home-based business?
- Do I want to work 5 days a week? 6 or 7?
- Do I want to be an absentee owner?
- Is there a specific industry I want to work in?

These questions and other critical ones can be found in the worksheet in Figure 3-1. I encourage you to complete it before looking at specific franchises. Once you have completed the worksheet, determine which factors are nonnegotiable and which are negotiable. In this way, you will set up a priorities list that will guide you through the decision process.

Deciding on Basics

An important choice that you will have to make, either as part of your priorities list or later when you've zeroed in on a particular industry or business, is the choice between a large, established franchise system and a small, newer one, or something between. This is an important decision, because the age and size of the system will impact on you in many ways.

Trap

Be careful if your choice is a very small or a very large franchise system. If there are only a few operating units, the franchisor may not have enough experience to make it work, and if the system is very large all the regions may be saturated and you'll have to settle for less than prime locations.

Answering these questions will give you a good start toward setting priorities for a franchise choice.

1. Where will the business be located? In the city, the suburbs, the countryside? _____

   _____

   _____

2. Do I want to commute? If so, what are the time limits? _____

   _____

   _____

3. Do I want a home-based business? _____

   _____

4. Do I want to work 5 days a week? 6 or 7? How many hours per day?_____

   _____

5. Do I want to be an absentee owner? _____

   _____

6. Is there a specific industry I want to work in?_____

   _____

7. Are there any industries, products, or services that I will not work with, under any circumstances? _____

   _____

   _____

8. Are there any specific characteristics that must exist in the business? _____

   _____

   _____

   (Continued)

Figure 3.1. Worksheet for Setting Priorities.

9. Do I want a product or a services franchise?_____

    _____

    _____

10. Do I want a new or an established system? _____

    _____

    _____

11. Do I want a large or small franchise system?_____

    _____

    _____

12. Do I want a system with slow and steady growth or a rapid-growth one?_____

    _____

    _____

13. Do I want the system to have company-owned stores?_____

    _____

    _____

14. What kind of attitude do I want in the franchisor? Paternalistic? Dictatorial? Collegial? Laid back? _____

    _____

    _____

15. How important is name recognition? On a regional or national basis? _____

    _____

    _____

16. How much can I pay for the franchise?_____

    _____

    _____

Figure 3-1. (*Continued*)

The Franchising Superstars

The highly visible, larger franchise systems, such as ITT Sheraton, Jiffy Lube, Dunkin' Donuts, Pizza Hut, and Century 21 Real Estate are likely to be well-capitalized and have a demonstrated track record and an experienced management staff. For the most part, they can be looked at as lower-risk investments.

Since they have a greater number of franchisees, more cooperative benefits will accrue to the new franchisee. This means a powerful advertising reach, better name and brand recognition, preferential treatment from suppliers and lower operating costs through volume purchasing.

Tip

One of the biggest reasons for choosing a known name franchise is *instant customers.*

But before you sign on the dotted line, consider also the downside of a big-name franchise. For one, the larger, mature franchises tend to be in flat markets with many competitors. More important for new franchisees, often few good locations are available. Then, too, participation in this lower risk opportunity usually means a very large entry cost.

On the operating side, these systems often become more authoritarian and bureaucratic as they grow. The corporation can get so enmeshed with administrative duties that it loses touch with its marketplace. Some franchisees feel lost in the shuffle while others have even the smallest decisions dictated to them by their franchisor.

Several of the fast-food franchisees we talked to emphatically stated that you get instant customers and nearly instant profit as well with a big name. But George Hayden, a Wendy's franchisee, says, "It still isn't for everybody. You must have the temperament to be able to deal with large bank debt to start the business." In addition, several franchisees mentioned the heavy degree of control exerted by the franchisor. One gave as an example a case where the fast-food restaurant needed another women's bathroom but the store size stipulated only one bathroom, so the franchisor refused to allow it.

One franchisee was critical of a large fast-food purveyor who only allows people who come up through their system to buy a franchise. Typically, the prospective franchisee comes out of college with no real business experience, and goes through the ranks, working at various jobs. The interviewed franchisee summed it up like this: The system is looking for a pliable person only trained in the franchisor's way of doing business.

The Rising Stars

About 70 percent of all franchise companies have fewer than 50 locations, so you'll have a bigger choice if you opt for the newer, smaller systems. However, just as with the name franchises, you will have a variety of negatives and positives to consider first.

One big feature is that the up-and-coming franchisor tends to be in an uncrowded industry which is not overrun with competitors. Ideally, the business is one recently deemed "hot," and prime locations and regions are still available. The initial charges and royalty fees are usually lower, and franchisors will often negotiate the terms of the transaction. The system management is usually flexible, not set in its ways, and encourages participation from the franchisees.

Tip

If you decide to be one of the first franchise operators for a new franchisor, negotiate hard. Your risk is proportionately higher and you should be compensated for this.

These benefits, however, are offset by some costs. The newer franchise poses a somewhat higher risk than the established one. For one thing, there's no demonstrated track record. The franchisors may not have worked out all the bugs in the system, and you'll have to experiment right along with them. Then, too, a small number of franchisees undoubtedly brings less advertising power—with a corresponding lack of name recognition—and usually higher wholesale prices for the franchisee.

Trap

Investigate the capitalization of a new franchise very thoroughly. If the franchisor is not well-capitalized, the entire program may collapse—and you along with it.

Once you have made a choice on the size of the franchise system, you might want to be even more specific. For example, if you prefer a smaller franchise system, you can set a number of operating units to act as a guideline. You will limit your choice to systems that have, say, 20 to 100 units. Conversely, if you find the larger systems more appealing, then you may set limits of no less than 500 or more than 2000 units.

Corporate Units

Size is just one of the priorities you may have. For instance, another crucial factor for some franchisees is whether the system operates company-owned stores. The conventional wisdom is that being in the thick of daily operations makes the franchisor more aware of the franchisee needs and can spawn ideas for improvements. However, in more than just a few cases franchisees have been hurt by corporate stores that have situated themselves too close to the franchisee's location and, in effect, taken away from the franchisee's business.

Tip

When you first meet with the franchisor, ask what its policy is on company-owned stores. If company units are operated, find out if distance restrictions apply. What is the closest distance allowed to franchisee units? Are the distances strictly adhered to? Is the policy written into the franchise contract? Does the franchisor have any immediate plans to open stores in your selected area?

Product versus Service Franchises

When you make your priorities list, you will probably give some thought to the choice between a product and a service franchise. In essence your choice comes down to this: Service franchises are riding a crest of popularity and are now the faster selling of the two types of franchises. However, selling services is a harder sell for the franchisee.

It is considerably harder to sell an intangible service than a tangible product. Your service can't be seen, smelled, touched, or tasted. Sales efforts must concentrate on the benefits a customer receives from the service. Quite often it is difficult to evaluate the quality of a service until the service is actually performed. With a product franchise, the product itself can communicate a value to the customer, and so customers feel more secure in their buying decision, making it an easier sell for the franchisee.

Some of the challenges you must consider with a service franchise:

- Your business location is more restricted to a particular location, since your market will probably be a very targetted one.

- The size of the operation is limited because customers will purchase your time and performance rather than a mass-produced product.

- Service quality is difficult to standardize because we deal with variations in human performance. Developing a consistency with each customer will take a special effort.

- Sales of services will depend greatly upon past customers who will give high recommendations.

As you can see from these few examples, you must consider many aspects of many questions before you can come up with your priority list. Your first priorities list will probably not be your last.

Matching Priorities to Opportunities

As we interviewed franchisees, we noted that the ones who seemed to be the most satisfied and happiest in their franchise choices were those who actively set up priorities. After a period of personal analysis and investigation, these franchisees came up with maybe five or six "must-haves" for their choice. Following are the stories of four franchisees and how they managed to match their priorities with the franchise opportunity.

Finding a Franchise with Low Start-Up Costs.   Arny Grushkin, based in Westport, Connecticut, was the president of a corporate subsidiary company when the economic downturn and company consolidation led to his leaving. After an unsuccessful job search, he explored independent business opportunities and then settled on franchising.

After giving it some thought, Grushkin sat down and wrote a profile of a franchise opportunity that would interest him. These were his priorities:

- No overhead
- No salaried employees
- Operate out of his house
- Not selling each day (some continuity from customers)
- Residual income possibility
- A newer franchise with prime areas available for franchising

Shortly after this, Grushkin attended one of the giant franchise shows and literally saw everything from "soup to nuts." At the very end of the show he came upon Unishippers, a concept of economical air shipments for small and moderate business users. Unishippers fulfilled his profile requirements, and a new franchisee was in business.

Entrepreneurial Qualities Influence Choice.   Steve Saffar was a successful automobile agency manager who did not really enjoy his work. He made a great salary, but he also worked very long hours, and he was itching to have the opportunity to produce for himself and exert a greater control over his life. Finally he looked at the opportunities in independent and franchise businesses. Choosing a franchise concept, he wrote out what he called his "guidelines" for the business. They were:

- Recession-proof business
- Repetitive in nature

- Not capital intensive
- Low overhead
- High degree of personal independence (no intensive franchisor "looking over your shoulder")

When Saffar found The Wedding Pages franchise, a wedding information publication that sells advertising, he found the right franchise for his guidelines.

When Regional Expansion Is a Priority.   When Linda Moore hit the glass ceiling and became annoyed with the widespread mismanagement at a *Fortune* 500 corporation, she thought this might be the time to strike out on her own. Like most former corporate employees, she considered both independent and franchise businesses.

Rejecting an independent business for a variety of reasons, she defined her ideal franchise opportunity in terms of what she wanted and what she didn't want:

- No high-tech businesses
- No food businesses
- Leaning toward a professional service
- System must be ethical and well-managed
- Opportunity to develop a business regionally not just operation of a store or two

Because Moore felt the regional development opportunity was an important criterion for her, her franchise system had to be relatively young—an entire region had to be available to her. A two-year-old franchise called Ledger Plus, a service which does accounting, tax planning, and preparation for small businesses, fit the bill, and Linda Moore is now a happy regional owner for the company.

Zeroing in on a Niche Business.   After Jay McDuffie decided he wasn't going to relocate with his company, he started to look at franchising. He used these guidelines in making his choice:

- Customers come to him (no making cold calls)
- A niche business, not one in a large industry with a lot of competition

- A repeat business
- No big loan required

McDuffie considered several businesses—quick printing, fast food, dry cleaning—all businesses where people would come to him and which would be repeat businesses. One by one, he eliminated these businesses, basically because each was too expensive to get into and each had too much competition. He eventually bought a franchise business called Check Express, a check-cashing business, which fit all his nonnegotiable guidelines.

Other Considerations in Choosing a System.   Several of the franchisees we talked to were not as formal in setting out their priorities, but they had a few overriding requirements that had to be met. Two of these stories follow.

Judy Gedman was a salesperson for software and hardware programs to businesses and left because of frustration with large corporations. She eventually chose a franchise in the sign industry, Fastsigns, because "it was creative, clean, computer oriented, and industry driven." In the choosing process Judy looked also at a retail card shop and a frozen yogurt shop. She rejected these because "your location makes or breaks you. I feel it's better to go out and market something." For Judy, the Fastsigns business afforded her better control of her fate.

A Citizens Against Crime franchisee presents free crime prevention seminars to businesses, rotaries, and other organizations. The franchisees make money by selling safety items during and after the programs. Nancy Mann, one of the franchisees, says many choose the franchise because they have had personal experiences with a crime and have then become interested in the preventive aspects. According to Nancy, "Citizens Against Crime is a franchise where you can both feel good and make money. There are many teachers, ministers, and social workers involved with the franchise." In this franchise, says Nancy, "You must care about people, not only about making money."

Poor Franchise Choices.   As you might expect, every franchisee we talked to didn't, in hindsight, make the best choice possible. Unfortunate choices in general resulted because the individual didn't analyze and investigate the various opportunities beforehand. The following franchisee story can give you an idea of how things can go wrong if the initial homework isn't done.

A franchisee in the retail frozen yogurt business says when he bought the first store he didn't understand what "retail" meant. Now, after opening six stores, he doesn't think he's really good at it. "You need to be able to size up customers, be able to predict what your customers will like or dislike, and create a certain retail atmosphere." Another problem which he did not anticipate in the business is the seasonal factor. The business falls off dramatically in the winter, and a cold winter heightens this effect. The net result is a serious cash flow problem for the franchisee during certain times of the year. If he could do it over, the franchisee would still buy a franchise, but he would look more carefully at his capabilities and the nature of the business itself and make a different choice.

Franchising from Home

One of the choices you will undoubtedly make is whether to look to businesses that are home-based or those that require an office or storefront. Although home-based businesses are gaining in popularity, analyze this option very carefully. To be sure, the usual gut reaction today when considering working from the home is, "Great! No more commuting, no more traffic jams, no boss, no time clock." Working from home seems to appeal to many people, but, like most of the other choices you'll make, this one requires careful thought. Certainly, working from the home is not for everyone.

Of the franchisees we interviewed, 24 percent ran home-based businesses which ranged from business services (e.g., Leadership Management Inc.) to cleaning services (e.g., Jani-King) and computer learning (e.g., Computertots). Their reactions to the home-based experience were mixed.

Sandi Vettle, a Leadership Management franchisee, and Fred Banty, a Padgett Business Services franchisee, both believe that an office environment is more conducive to business. Vettle began her business in her home and then switched to an office building where she found that a professional office setting improves her productivity. "Working from the home is fine only if you are a very disciplined person," says Vettle. Fred Banty also feels that an outside office is better for business, yet he remains home-based so he can be close to his three small children. Banty believes that an outside office would help with franchise name recognition and would present a more professional image. He also thinks there would be fewer distractions and business would increase if he moved out of the home.

Meanwhile, Mary Cunningham, a Decorating Den franchisee, staunchly supports the home-based option. She doesn't feel that her productivity at home is lessened. "I am very disciplined and usually work seven days a week," says Cunningham. She adds that she likes "working from the home better than from an office. I still deal with people all the time, but I don't have to put up with all the personality problems in the office."

Trap

When you live and work in the same space it's easy to feel claustrophobic. Schedule outside meetings, lunch dates, sales calls—activities that will get you away from the too-familiar setting on a regular basis.

Before making a decision on a home-based business, you will need to examine your personality, lifestyle, work habits, and motives. These are some of the questions you should ask yourself:

1. *Am I self-motivated?* Without the structure of a workplace you will need a good deal of discipline and motivation to set goals and objectives on a daily and long-term basis.

2. *Do I have a reason for wanting to work from home other than just saving money?* If saving money is your only motive, then you're not really choosing a home-based business. Chances are the money saved won't be enough to make you happy working at home, and you might better look at alternatives. Valid reasons for working at home include family obligations requiring flexible schedules, physical disabilities which inhibit movement, and a desire for a more independent lifestyle.

3. *Am I multitalented and resourceful?* Although all franchises require many skills, a home-based one will require even more juggling

of duties. You'll be the one to type the letters, send the faxes, make the sales call, and handle the filing.

4. *Am I comfortable working alone?* If you need to have people around you all the time to be happy and effective, the home-based option isn't for you. You should feel confident working on your own.

5. *Does your house have the necessary space and facilities for operation of a business?* You must have a sufficient work area which is not make-shift or temporary. In addition to office furniture, you will also need equipment, such as computers, fax machines, printers, and answering machines. You might also need storage space, as well as additional electrical circuits and extra phone lines.

6. *Will your family support your decision to operate a home-based franchise?* With family space overlapping business space, the entire family must understand that some areas will be out of bounds and that the privacy of the business area must be respected.

If you become part of the trend of operating a new, small business from your home, you will have an increasing variety of businesses to choose from. Businesses that can be started from a home location include financial services, residential and commercial cleaning services, direct mail, computer classes, and publishing businesses.

Trap

The biggest problem with working from home is not that you won't work enough, but that you will overwork! You'll be constantly reminded of projects to be completed and phone calls that need to be returned. It's possible to work all hours of the day, all week-long. Resist the temptation and put up a "business is closed" sign at the appropriate times.

Selecting Your Work Hours

Remember, in the introduction where we said that the ability to work hard is a given for readers of this book? Well, it's still a given, but if the number of hours worked is a priority for you, a nonnegotiable item, you should consider some things carefully.

In general, new franchisees say they work harder and longer hours than they ever did in their previous jobs. Most also say they work considerably longer hours than they expected, 80 hours a week in some cases. And, although many franchisees said the long hours left them feeling tired and worn-out, they also felt the long hours were necessary to build their businesses.

However, we find the time commitments differ, depending upon the type of business. So when making your initial choice, you should investigate this aspect carefully. In a general way, you'll find the following true for three of the main types of franchises:

Business service franchises. Most often you run the business the way you expect it to be run. The franchisor generally will not require adherence to a specific schedule. You will set the specific hours and days you work. This sort of franchise does give you a great deal of latitude and independence in terms of time management.

Retail business franchises. As a business operator in a mall or strip center, you will be required to follow its regulations. This usually implies long hours, maybe from 9 or 10 in the morning to 8 or 9 at night, and generally there is a 6- or 7-day work-week. There is little or no room for deviation in operating hours, so you are locked into a rigid schedule. You are given somewhat more latitude if your retail business is in a free-standing structure. You won't have mall developers or strip center operators to answer to.

Child-care franchises. This business normally coincides with school hours and parent's working hours. Child-care hours generally run from 6:30 a.m. to 6:30 p.m., and the centers can only close for a few national holidays. The trend seems to be toward adding extra hours for "nightcare" and "sick care," so it appears that hours may be getting even longer.

When considering the hours you would like to work compared to the requirements of a particular franchise business, there is one mitigating circumstance. Although some businesses have long hours and long work weeks "built-in," the demands on the franchise owner may be temporary. Many franchise owners tell of excruciating long hours the first few years of the business which change to reasonable work schedules as the business prospers and more employees are brought in.

Tip

Two of our interviewed franchisees advised: Try not to get too far away from things that you know. Don't get into something you know nothing about. Someone coming out of a corporation should probably not consider fast food franchises. It's just too big a change.

Five Hot Areas in Franchising

Unless you've decided to invest in a large, superstar franchise with a ready-made market, you'll probably explore various businesses looking for the ones in the "hottest" areas, the ones deemed most likely to succeed. The problem is that everyone doesn't necessarily agree on the best businesses to make more money more quickly. You'll have to be the ultimate judge on that.

In any case, I'm going to describe what I think are the five best growth areas in franchising. The five selections which follow are chosen because they capitalize on demographic, social, economic, and psychodynamic trends. I would expect these areas to remain relatively hot for at least the next decade:

1. *Business services.* Corporate downsizing has been a boon to business service franchises, and the trend is very likely to continue. The employees remaining at corporations are overworked and overstressed and need help. Hundreds of services once performed in-house are now being bought from outside businesses. Look for franchises with functions such as consulting, accounting, training programs, product design, corporate travel, legal services, data processing, voice messaging, advertising, and temporary help.

Tip

Think about this. A business service franchise could work very well with a *team* of owners—almost like a corporate business setting. It's a way to spread the operating responsibilities and the financial obligations and re-create a familiar setting for doing business.

2. *Child-related businesses.* It is estimated that about 30 million children under the age of 13 live in single-parent households where

the parent is working or in households where both parents work. This fact accounts for a good deal of the growth in child-related franchises. Look for franchises such as exercise gyms, nanny services, day-care centers, teaching programs (such as computer skills, foreign language skills, and help for learning problems).

3. *Elderly population products and services.* At the other end of the demographic spectrum, we have a growing aging population in the United States. As can be expected, look for franchises dealing with health care, such as in-home health care, medical products and distribution, and personnel agencies for health care workers. Travel and leisure activities, especially geared to an older population, are also flourishing from this trend.

4. *General services.* The boom in service franchises (other than business-to-business) is expected to continue unabated. The population has a disposable income but less and less time to spend it. Think about time-consuming tasks that could be subcontracted to service companies. Look for services such as cleaning, lawn care, decorating, car repairs while you work, laundry pick-up at work, and other time-saving services.

5. *Products and services that offer good value.* Consumers are still watching their spending, even if it is considered "postrecession." Thus franchises offering products and services that have a high perceived value will flourish. Look for restaurants and food services where food is plentiful and inexpensive or moderately priced. The double-drive-through restaurants are growing in number, for example, and should continue to prosper. In addition, a restaurant with a distinctive, festive atmosphere and good, plentiful food is a winning concept.

So, there you have it—the top five best franchise opportunities. Now here are three franchise areas that you should consider only with much caution before proceeding:

1. *The diet business.* According to the statistics in several popular magazines, more Americans are overweight, exercising less, and eating more cholesterol and fat-laden food than the previous year. Add to this the bad publicity about dieting—"diets just don't work"—and you have an industry in a severe downswing. This is not to say that

the diet business will never be vital again. It's just that diet franchising is not a good bet for the near future.

2. *Retail businesses operating out of malls or strip centers.* Most likely this is a warning you haven't heard before, but think not twice, but three times or more, before signing up for a business located in a mall or strip center. You need only to listen to those who have tried it and report that the mall or strip developers are a *bigger* factor than the franchise system in regulating hours and imposing regulations and restrictions. Mall developers' influence on your business is great but you have no control over the management of the mall. With an incompetent management the quality of the mall can be destroyed. Then, too, in many instances the developers are almost like your financial partners because of lease arrangements that stipulate an additional payment to the developer when the franchisee goes over an agreed-upon sales figure. In those cases, the leaseholders have the right to audit sales figures. So, consider such locations carefully before signing the lease.

3. *New, low-cost franchises with a very limited marketplace.* The old adage "if it sounds too good to be true, it probably is" most likely applies here. A crop of franchisors have turned up that promote the low-investment requirements of their franchise systems as the big selling point. Unfortunately, some potential franchisees are drawn to these low-cost franchises because they think if it doesn't work, they haven't lost too much money. Never think like that! If a business investment is worth your time, effort, and money (even a small amount), you owe it to yourself to pick the very best investment you can.

Final Words

Examine your needs, desires, and capabilities before you start to talk to franchisors. Write down your "nonnegotiables" and then begin to look at systems which fit your requirements.

4

How Can I Be Sure I Won't Lose Money?

Be patient. Don't settle for anything less than the right franchise in the right location.   **HAROLD SANCHEZ**
General Nutrition Center franchisee

No matter how much training and help the system gives you, the success is created by the owner.   **STUART RUBEN**
Money Mailer franchisee

How can you be sure not to lose money? You can *never* be sure you won't lose money, but you can greatly improve your chances of making money.

Draw up a list of your priorities and then start to investigate those franchises which best fit your priorities. Attending one of the giant franchise shows is an easy way to acquaint yourself with the realm of possibilities. Next, you should look at a reference book that lists the different franchise opportunities in all the different sectors. Make a list of the ones that you think fit your priorities and then start the investigation.

Starting the Investigation

You're going to contact the franchise systems you're interested in—either by talking to company representatives at one of the shows or by calling the reps on the phone. Undoubtedly, you will receive an information package from the company. Probably it will contain a letter, a brochure describing the business, and a qualifying questionnaire.

The next step is for the franchisor to send you the "Uniform Franchise Offering Circular" (UFOC) for the particular business. The UFOC originated as a response to the complaints of those who were exploited by unethical individuals and con artists in the 1960s and 1970s. Today franchises are regulated by law. The Federal Trade Commission (FTC) requires that certain information must be disclosed to potential franchisees before a contract can be signed or any payment made. The information is presented to the prospective franchisee in the form of a document—the UFOC.

The FTC requires franchisors in every state to provide a UFOC but, in addition, some states require that the offering must first be approved and registered by the state before it can be promoted to prospective franchise buyers. Those states are: California, Hawaii, Illinois, Indiana, Maryland, Michigan, Minnesota, New York, North Dakota, Oregon, Rhode Island, South Dakota, Virginia, Washington, Wisconsin. Certain states such as Illinois and Minnesota have even more stringent requirements for the franchisor. This in turn affords better protection for the prospective franchisee.

The UFOC contains 23 items of information and must be current as of the completion of the franchisor's most recent fiscal year. If there is a material change to the information in the document, the franchisor must make a revision (to be issued quarterly). The disclosure document must be given to a prospective franchisee at whichever occurs earlier—the first personal meeting of franchisor and prospective franchisee or ten working days prior to the execution of a contract or money payment to the franchisor.

Tip

Although the FTC requires that specific information is given to the prospective franchisee, note that the FTC does not check the contained information and will not vouch for its accuracy. Nothing will take the place of your own investigative activities.

The 23 items of information in a UFOC are as follows:

1. *The franchisor and any predecessor.* This section contains historical background material on the franchisor as well as any predecessors. It includes corporate and trade names, address, and principal place of business. A description of the franchise should include information such as the nature of the franchise and the business experience of the franchisor, including direct experience in a franchise.

2. *Identity and business experience of persons affiliated with the franchisor.* All names of individuals having significant responsibilities in the operation of the business or in support services provided to the franchisees must be disclosed. Information stating the person's current position in the company and business experience for the last five years is also included. If a marketing representative or franchise broker is involved, the same information is required.

3. *Litigation history.* Detailed information on criminal, civil, and administrative litigation involving any of the officers, owners, directors, and key executives of the company is disclosed here if the allegations or proceedings would concern the potential franchisee.

4. *Bankruptcy history.* The franchisor must disclose whether the company or its directors and officers have filed for bankruptcy during the past 15 years. Information on each action must be included.

5. *Franchisee's initial franchise fee and/or other initial payment.* This section states the franchise fee and any other initial payments to be made by the franchisee upon the execution of the franchise agreement. The section discloses the terms of payment and fees, the use of such monies, and whether the payment and fees are refundable in whole or in part.

6. *Other fees.* All other fees are detailed including royalties, advertising fees, insurance expenses, training costs, audit and account-

ing costs, consulting, leases, alteration costs, and any other fees associated with the franchise.

7. *Franchisee's estimated initial investment.* The estimated expenditures associated with the opening of a franchise are recounted with a high and low range given for real estate, construction, equipment, fixtures, permits, furnishings, signage, inventory, working capital, etc. This section should include to whom payment is made for the preceding, under what terms, and whether refund terms apply.

8. *Obligations of franchisee to purchase or lease from designated sources.* Any requirements that the franchisee must purchase goods, services, supplies, equipment, or insurance for the opening and/or operation of the franchise from a franchisor-designated source must be disclosed. Franchisors also disclose if they receive income from the approved suppliers as a result of purchases by franchisees.

9. *Obligations of franchisee to purchase or lease in accordance with specifications or from approved suppliers.* A further elaboration on supply sourcing, this section itemizes any responsibility of the franchisee to purchase or lease either from preapproved suppliers or according to franchisor specifications. Specifications for purchases are not normally included but pricing, discounts, and procedures to have suppliers approved by the franchisor are usually cited.

Tip

Two important questions that should be answered by the franchisor are: Is the franchisee obligated to buy all supplies from the franchisor? If not, do franchisee-chosen suppliers have to be approved?

10. *Financing arrangements.* Any financing programs which are offered either by the franchisor or its designates are described in this section.

11. *Obligations of franchisor: other supervision, assistance, or services.* This section describes the initial and ongoing service and support of the franchisor. Often it is divided into two parts—service obligations of the franchisor and services that may be performed by the franchisor. Some types of service and support described are training, advertising material, site selection, market research, and computer services.

12. *Territorial rights.* If the franchisor grants exclusive rights, the territory and the rights will be described in this section. Any conditions that the franchisee must meet to retain these rights as well as the rights of the franchisor are also disclosed.

13. *Trademarks, service marks, trade names, logo types, and commercial symbols.* The franchisor must disclose information regarding the registration of trademarks, service marks, trade names, logo types, and commercial symbols with the U.S. Patent and Trademark Office. Also, included is a list of states and countries in which the marks are registered and any limitations imposed on the franchisee for the use of these marks.

14. *Patents and copyrights.* This disclosure lists any patents and copyrights that may be involved in the operation of the franchise and that may cover trade secrets and confidential information.

15. *Obligation of the franchisee to participate in the operation of the franchise business.* If the franchisor requires the active participation of the franchisee in the operation of the business, it must be so stated. Terms and conditions of the participation should be defined.

16. *Restrictions on goods and services offered by franchisee.* Any limits or exclusions on goods and services which can be commercialized by the franchisor are stated in this section.

17. *Renewal, termination, repurchase, modification, and assignment of the franchise agreement and related information.* This, the longest and most complex section, covers the franchisor's requirements and the franchisee's options when a franchise is to be renewed, terminated, repurchased, modified, or assigned.

18. *Arrangements with public figures.* If the franchisor has any compensation or endorsement program with a public figure it must be disclosed. If the public figure is involved in the ownership or the management of the franchise, it must also be disclosed.

Trap

Don't get fooled into thinking a franchise is better than it is just because a celebrity is associated with it. Base your decision on your investigative analysis of the franchise.

19. *Actual, average, projected, or forecasted franchise sales, profits, or earnings.* There is an option here. Some franchisees will state that they do not furnish the actual, average, projected, or forecasted sales and earnings to prospective franchisees. If a franchisor does make a claim of sales, profits, or earnings, then the franchisor must fully describe the method by which the claim is made.

20. *Information regarding franchises of the franchisor.* The franchisor provides a summary of franchises sold, the number actually operating, the number of agreements signed but not in operation, and the number of company-owned units. Information on the number of franchises terminated or not renewed, with the causes for termination or nonrenewal, for the past three years is also required.

21. *Financial statements.* In this section there is a complete set of financial statements, usually a balance sheet for the fiscal year ended, an income statement, and changes in the financial position of the franchisor for the most recent three fiscal years. Most states require audited statements.

Tip

The financial statements of new franchise systems will probably not be very impressive, since they have had no opportunity to establish a track record. In this case, concentrate more on evaluating the business concept and the management.

22. *Franchise agreement and related documents.* A copy of the franchise document and any other document to be signed by the franchisee must be included as exhibits.

23. *Acknowledgement of receipt by a prospective franchisee.* Prospective franchisees are required to sign an acknowledgement that a disclosure document was received from the franchisor.

Trap

Don't fall for the franchisor who treats the UFOC as a company secret and requires that you visit corporate headquarters *prior* to seeing their UFOC. The UFOC should be analyzed carefully before contemplating a visit to corporate headquarters.

What the UFOC Tells You

Getting an accurate idea of the franchisor will require some reading between the lines and a lot of additional questions. Although the contents of the UFOC are prescribed, most franchisors will present only the *minimum* information needed to get by. For example, the operations of a franchisor's advertising fund is not a required disclosure. This means the prospective franchisee won't know how the advertising royalty will be used nor what the strategy is.

However, changes are afoot. New UFOC guidelines were adopted in 1993 which will go into effect no earlier than January 1, 1994, and no later than January 1, 1995. The following are some of the major changes in the UFOC according to Bret Lowell, an attorney specializing in franchise law at Brownstein Zeidman and Lore in Washington, D.C.:

■ *Litigation (item 3 on the UFOC).* Under current guidelines certain lawsuits and settlements of lawsuits are not required to be disclosed. The new guidelines will broaden the category appreciably. For example, under current guidelines litigation is required to be disclosed only if it is "material," meaning it is likely to influence a prospective franchisee or have a significant financial impact on the franchisor. The new guidelines require that litigation reported includes any action brought by a present or former franchisee or by a supplier or landlord to the system.

Tip

This change will, in all likelihood, result in the franchisor disclosing all the company's litigation history, no longer picking and choosing what to disclose. Read this section carefully and look especially for an excessive number of lawsuits by franchisees. That might indicate that a franchisor is not living up to its agreement. A red flag—franchisors which are involved in civil actions and/or expulsions from securities associations.

■ *Initial Fees (item 5).* The new guidelines add a requirement to disclose, if the initial franchise fee is not uniform, the average franchise fee paid in the prior fiscal year.

This is your green light to negotiate fees. A record of nonuniform franchise fees indicates a willingness on the part of the franchisor to negotiate.

- *Initial investment (item 7).* Under current guidelines the franchisor is required to estimate the initial cash investment for a new franchisee. The new guidelines expand this disclosure requirement. First, they call for disclosure of "all costs necessary to begin operation of the franchise and operate the franchise during the initial phase of the business." Second, franchisors must show how they arrived at those figures. Finally, three months will normally be considered the minimum reasonable period for the "initial phase" of operation.

Trap

Many franchisors currently use one month of costs in initial phase estimates. Determine the actual time (i.e., one month, three months) the franchisor assigns to the initial phase. If the startup time is underestimated, you will be underestimating the beginning costs as well.

- *Obligation to purchase or lease from approved sources or according to specifications (item 8).* The new guidelines require franchisors to disclose the total revenue generated by sales to franchisees, and the gross profit from the sales. All this information is to be taken from the franchisor's audited financial statements.

Tip

Review this section to find out if the franchisor or approved source is charging franchisees a fair price on products or services. Look at the gross profit of the franchisor or approved source on required purchases and leases to see if it is reasonable.

- *Obligation to purchase or lease from approved sources or according to specification (item 8).* Franchisors will be required to disclose whether they make available to franchisees the criteria for approval of new suppliers who are proposed by franchisees. Franchisors also must disclose the procedure for obtaining supplier approval, as well as the procedure for revoking approval, and the time frames for notice of approval and disapproval.

Trap

Franchisors are often adamant about the franchisee's use of their approved suppliers. The prudent franchise investor should compare alternate supply sources with the franchisor's approved ones for price and quality.

- *Franchisee's obligations (item 9).* The new UFOC guidelines require a cross-reference in the franchise agreement (or other ancillary agreements) for provisions which impose obligations on franchisees. Franchisors will need to respond to a standard list of 24 items (including site selection, training, fees, transfer) and state the obligation of the franchisee, if any.

- *Financing (item 10).* Franchisors must disclose not only the terms of financing offered by the franchise system but also any financing arranged by the franchisor with banks and other lenders. In addition, franchisors are required to state interest using annual percentage rate (APR) format. Finally, they must set a ceiling for any claim they would bring against a franchisee that defaults under a promissory note.

Tip

Franchisors that offer financial assistance to prospective franchisees provide a service. Just make sure that the terms and conditions of the system-sponsored financing is fair to the franchisee.

- *Franchisor's obligations: advertising funds (item 11).* This change requires a more detailed and extensive explanation of the source and use of advertising funds. Franchisors must describe:

How the various advertising funds (systemwide or regional) actually spent their money, including the percentage of expenditure per category, in the most recently concluded fiscal year

Whether the franchisor or any of its affiliates receives payment from the funds for providing goods or services to the funds

Whether the fund is audited and whether financial statements of the fund are available for review by the franchisee

Whether company-owned units must contribute to the funds and, if so, how much

Whether some franchisees are required to contribute at different rates than others

The percentage of the advertising fund spent on advertising that is principally a solicitation for the sale of franchises

Tip

When you examine a company's advertising program and strategy, look for clear-cut goals and effective use of funding. You don't want to find out that most of the advertising dollars go toward attracting other franchisees, not customers.

- *Franchisor's obligations: advertising and other cooperatives (item 11).* The new guidelines specifically require disclosure of whether advertising cooperatives (groups of franchisees in a particular area or region) operate from written governing documents and whether such documents are available to the franchisee. Also, under item 6, franchisors must disclose whether company-owned units have a vote in the decision of franchisee cooperatives to impose fees on franchisees. If company-owned units have controlling voting power—there are more company-owned units than franchised units in a particular territory—then the franchisor must disclose a range for the fees imposed by the cooperative.

- *Franchisor's obligations: computer databases (item 11).* The current guidelines, originally issued in 1975, don't deal with the use of computer technology. Now franchisors will disclose information about the company hardware and software systems—in nontechnical language. This includes disclosure of the principal functions of the database, its technical specifications, the types and amount of data on the system, the cost to the franchisee for access to the system, anticipated telecommunications charges, costs of up-grades, the franchisor's experience operating a computer net-work, whether software is custom or off-the-shelf, the amount of user support, how often the system is updated, and how often the system was "down" due to operating problems in the preceding fiscal year.

- *Franchisor's obligations: training (item 11).* They must describe, in a table, the specific subjects covered in training and the hours spent on each subject in classroom study and on-the-job training.

- *Franchisor's obligations: operating manual (item 11).* Franchisors must include in the UFOC the table of contents from their operat-ing manual. Also, they will state the number of pages devoted to each subject and the total number of pages in the manual.

Trap

The operating manual is the blueprint of the business. Be alert to systems that do not have extensive manuals to guide franchisees.

- *Renewal, termination, transfer, and dispute resolution (item 17).* Fran-chisors are required to cross-reference 23 categories of informa-tion from the franchise agreement which must be put into a table. Franchisors must have clearly written, well-organized, and com-prehensive contracts to competently fulfill this disclosure.

- *Financial statements (item 21).* The new guidelines require a two-year comparative format and not only balance sheets and income statements but also statements of operations, stockholders' equity, and cash flows.

This is a lot of new information to peruse and analyze. But the net result of all these changes to the UFOC is that *you, the potential fran-chisee, will be better informed and protected. To get back to the original ques-tion of this chapter, "how can I be sure I won't lose money?"—These new guidelines will help a lot.*

An FTC survey found that prospective franchisees were most interested in the financial items of the Uniform Franchise Offering Circular, *but* it is hazardous not to read the entire document very carefully. Supplier sources, advertising fund use, training, hardware and software programs, and site selection, to name just a few considerations, are also extremely important and are prime ingredients for the franchisee's success.

Items for Closer Investigation

The People Behind the Franchise.   Check in the UFOC to see if the principals have the experience necessary to manage and operate the franchise system. Of course, if you are very serious about the franchise, you will visit the franchise headquarters and meet the principals in person. At this time you can get a further impression of the management's competency level.

Current Financial Condition of the Franchisor.   As per the new directives for item 21 of the UFOC, franchisors will be required to provide more than balance sheets and income statements. Use this information to determine the financial strength of the franchisor. Ascertain whether the franchisor is a public or private company. If it is a subsidiary of a larger company, find out if the parent company stands behind the franchisor financially.

Company-Owned Stores.   Your assignment is to find out if the stores are voluntarily owned company stores or reacquired units from struggling franchisees. Franchisors often try to hide the number of failed units by buying them back for use as company stores. Ask if they're for sale, and, if they're not, you'll know that they are legitimate, company-owned stores.

Market Strength and Competition.   Unfortunately, the UFOC does not include an assessment of the company's market share and competitors. However, officers of the franchise system should be able to give you a pretty fair idea of how the company fares relative to its competition. Try to determine how strong the marketing efforts are, especially in terms of name recognition. If you're looking at a new company with virtually no name recognition, find out how they plan to gain name recognition in the future. If no one can give you a satisfactory answer to these questions, maybe you'd better look elsewhere.

Trap

Find out the marketing plans of the franchisor. Ask if it now sells or plans to sell products or services through a distribution channel other than the franchises. For example, a franchisor might sell its products through a grocery chain and end up competing with its franchisees.

Franchisor's Plan for the Next Five Years.   When meeting with the franchise principals, you should ask them what their plans are for the next five years. First of all, you want to be sure they have a well-thought-out, comprehensive, long-term strategy and are not operating by the seat of their pants. It is also important to you as a franchisee to know the franchisor's plans for expansion, whether it plans to operate internationally and whether it plans to add new products or services. All this can impact on your business. Find out if the franchisor is keeping up with changes in the industry. You may want to ask if a research and development (R&D) department or its informal equivalent exists in the company.

Trap

Pay close attention to the franchisor's plan for growth. Beware of a franchise system which grows at an unmanageable rate. Not only does the servicing of franchisees suffer, but the system tends to lose contact with the marketplace which made it successful in the first place. It's far better for you to choose a franchise which plans to grow at a manageable rate, making sure quality and control of the system never suffers.

Tip

One of the very, very *best* ways to be sure you won't lose money is to work in the franchise before buying. Some prospective franchisees work in the franchise for no money—just to be sure there are no big surprises when they sign the contract!

Location, Location, Location

Here's one important bit of information you must never forget: *A poorly selected site for a franchise will most likely mean failure—even if the concept is great!* And since this chapter is dedicated to ways to be sure that you don't lose money, choosing the location of your franchise business is of prime importance.

The location of a fast-food business can make or break it. Camille and Edward DiNapoli, Subway franchisees, feel that location is by far the most important aspect of the business. Before opening, Camille and her husband spent a lot of time looking at the neighborhood demographics and especially at the traffic patterns and parking facilities. One neighboring franchisee is struggling because there is almost no parking available for the shop, although all other factors are acceptable.

Tip

Don't overlook the obvious when picking a location. Customers are not going to ride around and around looking for a space to park so they can use your products or services.

However, for some types of franchises, location is less important. Let's say you wanted to open a tax and accounting service. You still would conduct marketing and demographic assessments to situate yourself in an area where there is a market demand. But since you would often be traveling to the customer's place of business and since you don't rely on foot traffic, the convenience of your location isn't as critical.

Tip

College campuses can be great locations for service businesses. Poll students first to determine which services they need and want on campus. This almost ensures success!

Don't be so eager to open your franchise that you don't spend enough time looking at and assessing locations. Harold Sanchez, a GNC (General Nutrition Center—a retail health products store) franchisee, made that mistake. He says, "I got nudgy to get into business after taking a separation package from my corporation and took a location that the franchisor had settled on even though I had grave misgivings about it." Now Sanchez realizes that his business will not reach its full potential at the present location, and he is contemplating the expense and trouble of moving it elsewhere.

The type of structure best for your business will also be a determinant of the location. Sometimes personal preference is the decisive factor here. For example, Jeff Grayson has a different setup with each of his Pizzeria Uno restaurants. One restaurant is in an indoor mall, one is in a strip center, and one is freestanding. Grayson likes the freestanding best of all. He says, "It's individualistic and you're not hit with the percentage rates (on rents) that you have in malls and centers." (For help in choosing a location, fill out the site selection worksheet in Figure 4-5 at the end of the chapter.)

Tip

Think about opening your franchise on a military base if your products and services are appropriate. This ready-made market proved just right for a KFC franchise on a U.S. Army base in Fort Campbell, Kentucky, and a Domino's Pizza franchise on a U.S. Marine base in California. The KFC franchisee is the biggest grossing franchise for the system in the United States, and the Domino's franchisee sells the most Domino's pizzas in the United States.

Quizzing Current Franchisees

After you have read and analyzed a franchisor's offering document (the UFOC), then it's time to start telephoning if you are still interested in pursuing the opportunity. You'll be calling or visiting franchisees and plying them with questions. *This is a step you can't skip!*

Turn to the exhibit section of the UFOC, where most franchisors include a list of franchisees, complete with name, address, and telephone number. If this information is not included, the franchisor should furnish it to you upon your request. In addition, most fran-

chisors list franchisees "who have been terminated, canceled, not renewed or have voluntarily or involuntarily ceased to operate the
business during the current year."

It's difficult to give an *absolute* number that must be called. The
size of the system has a lot to do with it. If there are only five franchisees, you should call all five. But in the larger systems, you'll have to
use your judgment. Try to get a good cross-section of franchisees,
and don't forget to call several of the franchisees who voluntarily or
involuntarily left the system.

What will you talk to them about? You'll ask them about all the
things that are important to you. Glenn and Connie Schenenga, Future Kids (computer training) franchisees, spoke to a great many of
the 40 or 50 franchisees listed and asked them questions like, "Are
you making any money? Are you happy? What are the positives and
negatives of the business?" Pretty basic questions, but ones that every
prospective franchisee would like to know the answers to. You might
also inquire about the hours involved in running the business, the
relationship of franchisee and franchisor and, of course, when the
franchisees turned their first profit.

If you contact a wide cross-section, you will undoubtedly encounter struggling, surviving, successful, and supersuccessful franchisees.
Try to determine, as best you can, why some are not succeeding. Is
the franchisee taking advantage of the corporate support? Is the
franchisee putting in the time? Perhaps the owner is an absentee
one. Is the franchisee out selling? The point is to try and find out if
the problems lie with the franchisee or the franchise system.

Calculating Potential Sales, Cash Flow, and Profit

Calculating the potential sales, cash flow, and profit of a franchise
business is a key element in choosing a profit-making franchise. This
job is not always as easy as it should be. Neither the Federal Trade
Commission (FTC) nor any of the states require a franchisor to tell
how well franchisees have done in the past or estimate how much a
new franchisee is likely to earn. However, franchisors are allowed to
provide a voluntary written "earnings claim" in their offering circu-

lar. In 1992, about 32 percent of franchisors chose to make this voluntary statement (up from 18 percent in 1991). The good news is that competitive pressures will certainly continue to increase the number of franchisors that include earnings claims.

Your chosen franchise business should supply you with some figures of average sales in the franchisee units. Figure 4-1 is an example of how one franchisor, Parcel Plus, a shipping, business and com-

---

Item XIX

Representations Regarding Earning Capability

Gross Sales of Franchised Units
in Operation at Least One Year

As of December 31, 1992

Number of Units in Sample: 47
Arithmetic Average Annual Sales: $184,050
Median Average Annual Sales: $175,300
Range of Sales for Top Seven Stores: $322,187 to $447,590
Range of Sales for Bottom Seven Stores: $77,021 to $96,647

Average Sales by State

State	No. of Units	Total Sales	Average Annual Sales
California	2	$ 682,966	341,483
Connecticut	1	93,825	93,825
Delaware	1	96,647	96,647
District of Columbia	1	218,751	218,751
Maryland	19	3,537,648	186,192
Massachusetts	3	364,095	121,365
New Hampshire	2	298,044	149,022
Pennsylvania	1	235,013	235,013
Virginia	17	3,123,342	183,726
Total Units	47	$8,650,331	$184,050

Figure 4-1. Sample Franchisor Earning Claim. (*PARCEL PLUS, 2666 Riva Road, Suite 120, Annapolis, Maryland 21401-7351.*)

puter support service business, gets this information to its prospective franchisees.

Many franchisors have withheld earnings claims because they fear lawsuits in the event that the projections fall short. Unfortunately, this means franchise investors have to take a roundabout way to come up with the appropriate numbers.

Calculating Average Gross Sales

One way to calculate average gross sales per franchisee when no earnings claim is available is the following:

1. Check the franchisor's audited financials for the total royalty payment paid to them from franchisees.

2. Find in the offering document the percentage of gross sales the franchisees pay out as royalties (the royalty rate).

3. Calculate the number of full-time operating franchises. Exclude the company-owned stores from this total.

4. Divide the total royalty payments by the number of franchisees. *This is the average royalty payment per franchisee.*

5. Then divide this number by the royalty rate to calculate the *average gross sale per franchisee.*

Let's take a simple example to show you how this works. The franchisor shows $2 million in royalty payments from franchisees in its financial statements. The system has 100 operating franchises and two company stores. So we will divide $2 million (total royalty) by 100 and we find that $20,000 is the average royalty payment. The royalty rate is 5 percent. We then divide 20,000 by 0.05 (5 percent) and find that $400,000 is the average gross sale per franchisee. (Refer to Figure 4-2 to help with your calculations.)

Projecting Cash Flow

Cash flow is the difference between what your business takes in and what you spend. The technique used to anticipate cash needs is called a "cash flow analysis," and it will tell you when you are likely to

1. Total Royalty Amount franchisor receives from franchisees
   $_____

2. Royalty Rate _____%

3. Number of Operating Franchises (No company stores)

   _____

4. Total Royalty Paid (#1) divided by Number of Franchisees (#3)
   = Average Royalty Payment per franchisee

5. Average Royalty Payment per franchisee divided by the Royalty
   Rate (#2) = Average Gross Sales per franchisee

Figure 4-2. Worksheet for Average Gross Sales per Franchisee.

have a shortage as well as a surplus of cash. Your purpose in putting
together these cash flow numbers is to get a picture of whether your
working capital is sufficient to operate the business.

Let's say your initial investment for XYZ franchise is $50,000 and
that includes the franchise fee and start-up equipment, furniture,
and rent. You have $70,000 ($40,000 from a home equity loan, and
$30,000 from your savings) so this leaves you with $20,000 for *operating or working capital*. Then what you will want to determine is: Will
the $20,000 be enough to get the business through the startup phase
or will there be a shortfall—necessitating a scramble for more funds?

Where do you start? You start by looking at the projected annual
sales. (That's why it's very important that the franchisor supply you
with this very basic historical information.) Let's say average sales in
your state (or region) for the chosen franchise is $250,000. To pro-
ject your cash flow needs you can simply divide the figure by 12 and
you will have an estimated monthly sales figure. If, however, by talking to present franchisees, you know that there is a seasonal skew—

sales are not evenly balanced throughout the year—you should work this into your projections.

Interestingly enough, some major fast food franchisees we interviewed said there was even a seasonality in their business. They had heavier sales in the spring and summer seasons. Of course, if you're in the business of preparing taxes you can project your busiest period to be the first third of the year. So if you detect a seasonality to the proposed business, build this into your projections by showing greater sales figures at some times of the year and, of course, less than one-twelfth of the total in other months.

After you have estimated sales for each month of the year, you will need this additional information:

1. If you're buying a cash business, you already have your cash receipts each month from your estimated sales figure. If, however, you will be extending credit to customers, there will be a time lapse between the time of the sale and the time that the funds are deposited in your bank account.

Trap

The time lag between making the sale and collecting the money is the reason most businesses get into cash flow problems. You will have to pay your suppliers for goods and services even if you're not paid on time. If your business is known for slow-paying customers (find out from other franchisees), calculate that you may need double the working capital you anticipated.

2. If your business extends credit, then you must put the credit terms into your projections. For example, if your credit terms are net invoice payable in 30 days, you will show a sale in January, for example, but the receivable will be noted as paid in February. If you want to see more of the downside, show payment in March, allowing for late payments.

3. Then you must make a list of expenditures (cash outlays) for the month. This includes: cost of goods/purchases (get the figures from the franchisor); rent; loan payments; payroll; supplies; advertising; telephone; utilities; insurance; royalty to franchisor; and other

miscellaneous payments. You may want to split the expenditures into two types: fixed monthly payments such as rent, and variable payments such as royalties.

4. Now you simply add up the incoming cash and collections for *total cash available*. Then add up all the monthly expenditures for *total cash paid out*. Finally, subtract the total cash paid out from the total cash available, and you will have your *cash position* or *net cash available*. (If you do not intend to take a monthly cash distribution at first and if you have no debt to service, stop right here.)

5. From the net cash available, you will then subtract your salary (distribution to owner). Then subtract the debt service amount (loan amortization) for the ending cash balance.

When you're all finished with your calculations, analyze the results. If the cash position comes up negative several times and you can't increase your working capital, you might need to rethink your choice of franchise investment. (See Figure 4-3 for a sample cash flow setup.)

Tip

If you are completely unfamiliar with cash flow projections or don't feel confident enough to put together a projection, do it with your accountant. In any case, don't skip this very important part of your franchise analysis.

Profit and Loss Statement

Lastly, you'll put together a projected profit and loss (P&L) statement for a two-year period. The good news is that most of the numbers are already there if you have already calculated annual sales and made the cash flow projections.

For your P&L statement, do the following:

1. Take your anticipated first-year sales and subtract from that the cost of the sales or the cost of the goods sold. Cost of goods sold are equal to the beginning inventory plus the purchases less the ending inventory. This gives you your *gross margin* number.

	Jan.	Feb.	Mar.	Apr.	May	June	July	Aug.	Sept.	Oct.	Nov.	Dec.	Year 1 total	Year 2 total
1. Beginning cash	30,000	5,734	7,031	8,328	10,125	10,172	10,218	11,140	9,625	8,109	5,218	6,265	30,000	7,312
Plus:														
2. Cash sales	14,000	14,000	14,000	13,000	13,000	13,000	12,000	12,000	12,000	14,000	16,000	18,000	165,000	181,500
3. Credit sales	0	7,500	7,500	7,500	6,500	6,500	6,500	5,000	5,000	5,000	7,500	8,500	73,000	92,528
4. Bank loan	40,000												40,000	
5. Total cash available	84,000	27,234	28,531	28,828	29,625	29,672	28,718	28,140	26,625	27,109	28,718	32,765	308,000	281,340
6. Purchases	16,125	8,063	8,063	6,563	7,313	7,313	5,438	6,375	6,375	9,750	10,313	13,313	105,000	115,500
7. Wages, including taxes	4,821	4,821	4,821	4,821	4,821	4,821	4,821	4,821	4,821	4,821	4,821	4,821	57,852	57,852
8. Supplies	75	75	75	75	75	75	75	75	75	75	75	75	900	900
9. Advertising	150	150	150	150	150	150	150	150	150	150	150	150	1,800	1,800
10. Rent	2,400	2,400	2,400	2,400	2,400	2,400	2,400	2,400	2,400	2,400	2,400	2,400	28,800	28,800
11. Real estate taxes	75	75	75	75	75	75	75	75	75	75	75	75	900	900
12. Telephone, electricity	520	520	520	520	520	520	520	520	520	520	520	520	6,240	6,240
13. Insurance	350	350	350	350	350	350	350	350	350	350	350	350	4,200	4,200
14. Interest	267	267	267	267	267	267	267	267	267	267	267	267	3,200	3,200
15. Royalty	430	430	430	390	390	390	340	340	340	430	490	600	5,000	
16. Miscellaneous	1,320	2,320	2,320	2,360	2,360	2,360	2,410	2,410	2,410	2,320	2,260	2,150	27,000	33,000
17. Franchise fee	25,000												25,000	
18. Startup equipment etc.	25,000												25,000	
19. Total cash expenditure	76,533	19,470	19,470	17,970	18,720	18,720	16,845	17,783	17,783	21,158	21,720	24,720	290,892	252,392
20. Net cash available	7,467	7,764	9,061	10,858	10,905	10,951	11,873	10,358	8,842	5,951	6,998	8,045	17,108	28,948
21. Distribution to owner	500	500	500	500	500	500	500	500	500	500	500	500	6,000	12,000
22. Loan fee	1,000												1,000	
23. Loan amortization	233	233	233	233	233	233	233	233	233	233	233	233	2,796	2,796
24. Ending cash balance	5,734	7,031	8,328	10,125	10,172	10,218	11,140	9,625	8,109	5,218	6,265	7,312	7,312	14,152
Loan balance	39,767	39,534	39,301	39,068	38,835	38,602	38,369	38,136	37,903	37,670	37,437	37,204	37,204	34,408

Figure 4-3. Cash Flow Statement—Best Franchise Inc. (*Dan Lasman, Hampstead Partners Inc., Wilton, CT.*)

64

2. Next add up all your expenditures for the year from your cash flow statement; this number will be your *total expenses*. Be sure to add accrued expenses plus noncash expenses such as depreciation. To better understand this part of the P&L statement, two definitions are necessary: *Depreciation* and *amortization* are sister concepts, with the distinction that depreciation deals with tangible assets and amortization with intangible assets. The concept of allocating the cost of a tangible asset over its useful life is depreciation. For example, if a company buys a machine for $1 million and the machinery has a useful life of five years, the machinery is depreciated or "expensed" over a period of five years at a rate of $200,000 per year. Amortization refers to the allocation of the cost of an intangible asset over its useful life. For example, if an individual buys a franchise and pays a franchise fee of $200,000, the franchise fee would probably be amortized over five years at a rate of $40,000 per year. (In the case of our example, Figure 4-4, the start-up equipment cost of $25,000 is being depreciated over five years. The franchise fee of $25,000 is being amortized over a period of five years as well. Note that the numbers are rounded off to the nearest dollar amount.)

3. When you subtract your total expenses from your gross profit, the number remaining is the *net income or loss before taxes*.

4. To do the second-year P&L projections, simply project a fair increase in sales (talk to present franchisees in the system for an estimated increase) and a corresponding increase in cost of sales. Expenditures will in some cases remain the same—rent, insurance, and maybe advertising—and others may increase, most likely payroll, royalty, perhaps telephone. In any case, make an informed judgment on these items, subtract the two figures, and you'll have *net income or loss before taxes for the second year*. Ideally, you'll be seeing a larger income or profit figure in the second year.

Why must you go through all these financial exercises? Though painstaking, they can show you whether the financial investment makes sound financial sense. If the numbers come out less than satisfactory and you go ahead anyway (maybe because you fall in love with the business), you may find yourself working long, demanding hours with little in the way of salary or profit to show for it.

	Jan.	Feb.	Mar.	Apr.	May	June	July	Aug.	Sept.	Oct.	Nov.	Dec.	Year 1 total	Year 2 total
Cash sales	14,000	14,000	14,000	13,000	13,000	13,000	12,000	12,000	12,000	14,000	16,000	18,000	165,000	181,500
Credit sales	7,500	7,500	7,500	6,500	6,500	6,500	5,000	5,000	5,000	7,500	8,500	12,000	85,000	93,500
Total sales	21,500	21,500	21,500	19,500	19,500	19,500	17,000	17,000	17,000	21,500	24,500	30,000	250,000	275,000
Cost of goods sold:														
Beginning inventory	0	8,063	8,063	8,063	7,313	7,313	7,313	6,375	6,375	6,375	8,063	9,188	0	11,250
Purchases	16,125	8,063	8,063	6,563	7,313	7,313	5,438	6,375	6,375	9,750	10,313	13,313	105,000	115,500
Goods available	16,125	16,125	16,125	14,625	14,625	14,625	12,750	12,750	12,750	16,125	18,375	22,500	105,000	126,750
(Less ending inventory)	(8,063)	(8,063)	(8,063)	(7,313)	(7,313)	(7,313)	(6,375)	(6,375)	(6,375)	(8,063)	(9,188)	(11,250)	(11,250)	(12,375)
Cost of goods sold	8,063	8,063	8,063	7,313	7,313	7,313	6,375	6,375	6,375	8,063	9,188	11,250	93,750	114,375
Gross margin	13,438	13,438	13,438	12,188	12,188	12,188	10,625	10,625	10,625	13,438	15,313	18,750	156,250	160,625
Operating expenses:														
Wages, including taxes	4,821	4,821	4,821	4,821	4,821	4,821	4,821	4,821	4,821	4,821	4,821	4,821	57,852	57,852
Supplies	75	75	75	75	75	75	75	75	75	75	75	75	900	900
Advertising	150	150	150	150	150	150	150	150	150	150	150	150	1,800	1,800
Rent	2,400	2,400	2,400	2,400	2,400	2,400	2,400	2,400	2,400	2,400	2,400	2,400	28,800	28,800
Real estate taxes	75	75	75	75	75	75	75	75	75	75	75	75	900	900
Telephone, electricity	520	520	520	520	520	520	520	520	520	520	520	520	6,240	6,240
Insurance	350	350	350	350	350	350	350	350	350	350	350	350	4,200	4,200
Royalty	430	430	430	390	390	390	340	340	340	430	490	600	5,000	5,000
Miscellaneous	2,320	2,320	2,320	2,360	2,360	2,360	2,410	2,410	2,140	2,320	2,260	2,150	28,000	28,000
Depreciation & Amortization	833	833	833	833	833	833	833	833	833	833	833	833	9,996	9,996
Total operating expenses	11,974	11,974	11,974	11,974	11,974	11,974	11,974	11,974	11,974	11,974	11,974	11,974	143,688	143,688
Operating income	1,464	1,464	1,464	214	214	214	(1,349)	(1,349)	(1,349)	1,464	3,339	6,776	12,562	16,937
Interest	267	267	267	267	267	267	267	267	267	267	267	267	3,204	2,976
Net income/(loss)	1,197	1,197	1,197	(54)	(54)	(54)	(1,616)	(1,616)	(1,616)	1,197	3,072	6,509	9,358	13,961

Figure 4-4. Profit and Loss Statement—Best Franchise Inc. (Dan Lasman, Hampstead Partners Inc., Wilton, Ct.)

Final Words

Investigating a franchise opportunity is time consuming and may require some help from an accountant or other competent financial person. Unfortunately, I know of no shortcuts, but I do know that if you carefully follow the steps outlined in this chapter and act accordingly, you probably won't lose money in a franchise investment.

1. General Information
   a. Site Location
   Address: _____
   State: _____ Zip: _____
   Frontage: _____ Depth: _____ Square Footage: _____
   Dimensions: Front: _____ Rear: _____ Left: _____ Rear: ____
   Tax Map and Tax Assessment Numbers: _____
   _____

   b. Seller/Landlord
   Name: _____
   Tax ID#: _____
   Address: _____
   State: _____ Zip: _____
   Telephone: (   ) _____ Fax: (   ) _____

   c. Seller/Landlord's Attorney
   Name: _____
   Address: _____
   State: _____ Zip: _____
   Telephone: (   ) _____ Fax: (   ) _____

   d. Listing Broker
   Name: _____
   Address: _____
   State: _____ Zip: _____
   Telephone: (   ) _____ Fax: (   ) _____

   e. Surveyor/Engineer
   Name: _____
   Address: _____
   State: _____ Zip: _____
   Telephone: (   ) _____ Fax: (   ) _____

Figure 4-5. Franchise System Site Selection Worksheet. (*Carl Carlsson, managing director, Franchise Business USA, Spotsylvania, Va.*)

2. Legal Data
   a. Legal Description
   b. Covenants and Restrictions

3. Site Characteristics
   a. Site Sketch

   b. Improvements
      (1) What improvements are on the site: Will demolition be required?
      (2) Does the site need cut or fill?
      (3) Will permits be needed for soil disturbance and erosion control?

   c. Site Utility Data

Service	*Line Size*	*On Site*	*Distance to Hook-Up*
Gas			
Sewer			
Water			
Electrical			
Telephone			
Storm Sewer			

   d. Site without Central Sewer and Water
   Is a septic system permitted? If so, has the Health Department issued a permit for a septic system?

   e. Storm Water Management
   Does the jurisdiction require a storm water management plan, or can the site be surface drained? Must the run-off be held on-site?

   f. Contaminated Soil
   Has the site ever been used as a gas station, for oil or chemical storage, a landfill, an auto salvage yard or similar use?

   (Continued)

Figure 4-5. *(Continued)*

g. Easements
Will it be necessary to negotiate any easements external of the site?

h. The Subdivision Process
Will a subdivision, consolidated plat, or similar work be required?

4. Zoning
   a. Current Zoning

   b. Special Exceptions, Variances, and Approvals
   What is the estimated time to secure the requisite special exceptions, permits, and approvals for a fast food drive-thru restaurant?

5. Signage
   a. Freestanding Pole Signs
      (1) Is a freestanding pole sign permitted? How is the square footage of the sign's surface area calculated?
      (2) What is the maximum permitted height of a free-standing pole sign?

   b. Roof and Building Signs
      (1) Are roof signs which give the building corporate identity permitted?
      (2) What factors govern the square footage of a sign's surface area when it is a part of the roof structure?

   c. Off-Premise Signs and Highway Billboards
   Are off-premise signs and billboards permitted?

6. Roadway and Traffic Data
   a. Primary Street
      (1) Number of Traffic Lanes and Speed Limit
      (2) One-way Roadway or Two-way

Figure 4-5. *(Continued)*

      (3) Daily Traffic Count—Date Taken and Source
      (4) Traffic Patterns and Ingress and Egress

  b. Secondary Street
      (1) Number of Traffic Lanes and Speed Limit
      (2) One-way Roadway or Two-way
      (3) Daily Traffic Count—Date Taken and Source
      (4) Traffic Patterns and Ingress and Egress

  c. Divider and Median Barriers
      (1) Does the roadway have a divider or median barrier?
      (2) What effect will the divider or median barrier have on access to the site?
      (3) Can crossovers be constructed? Outline the process and include estimated permit and construction costs.
      (4) What is the site's distance from existing crossovers?
      (5) Are there any ongoing or future changes planned for the roadway?
      (6) What is the process for securing curb cuts into the site?

  d. Deceleration/Acceleration Lanes

  e. Roadway Sketch: Show median strips, ingress, and egress.

7. Tax Data
  a. Special Assessments

  b. Tax Jurisdiction: When are taxes due, and what are the tax account and tax map numbers of the proposed site?

8. Educational Institutions (within 3 miles of proposed site)

9. Competitors (within 3 miles of proposed site)
  a. National and Regional Competitors
      Name: _____

      _____ Distance from Site _____

(Continued)

Figure 4-5. *(Continued)*

10. Customer Generators
    a. Shopping Generators—Major Malls and Strip Center
       Name: _____
       _____ Distance from Site _____

    b. Major Employment Generators
       Name: _____
       _____ Distance from Site _____

    c. Other Generators and Draws—List all located within site's
       trade area.

11. Financial Considerations
    a. Purchase Terms by Franchisor to Build for Franchisee's
       Use
       (1) Purchase Price: $ _____
       (2) Cost per Square Foot: $ _____
       (3) Summary of Sale Terms and Conditions: _____
           _____
           _____

    b. Lease Terms
       (1) Initial Base Rent: $ _____
       (2) Periodic Increases (Percentages): _____
       (3) Fit-up Contributions, Site Work, and Landlord Im-
           provements: _____
           _____
           _____
       (4) Initial Term: _____ Years. Options Terms Exercis-
           able for: _____ Years at $_____ per Month.

Figure 4-5. *(Continued)*

5

The Franchise Agreement: The Potential Deal Breaker

The franchise system can be likened to a cookbook. You may need to change the recipes a little. But if you want to change it entirely you shouldn't buy the cookbook.

RICK PETERSEN
Interim Healthcare franchisee

The first chapter told you something you may have found surprising—that you are not purchasing a franchise. You are leasing it. When I discussed this with Bret Lowell, a franchise attorney with Brownstein Zeidman and Lore, he characterized it in a slightly different way. Lowell says you are "often buying a limited opportunity" with an initial duration of 5 years or 10 years which may then go through 2 or 3 renewals. He did agree, however, that in many regards it is like a lease. The franchise agreement discusses fees, term, renewals, termination, and other elements found in most leases.

When you sign the franchise agreement, you have agreed to make payments and assume obligations in exchange for the use of a trade name and logo and a demonstrated formula for success. The franchise operating manual contains the formula. This manual covers everything the franchisee needs to know to do business. It documents the standards and policies that all franchisees are to follow. The manual is "loaned" to the franchisee for the term of the franchise agreement. Upon the expiration or termination of the agreement the book must be returned to the franchisor.

Is Anything in the Agreement Negotiable?

There is very little latitude for change in most franchising agreements. "Historically, the franchise systems have said that the agreement can't be changed because then the disclosure document won't match up," says Bret Lowell. Continuing, he adds, "A negotiated change that benefits the franchisee and doesn't challenge the disclosure document (UFOC) is now okay."

Lisa Brumm, a Formals Etc. franchisee (rented formal wear) felt that because her chosen franchise was at a very early stage, some things should be negotiable. She had heard franchisors claiming they couldn't change things in the contract on a case-by-case basis because they would have to re-register with the state if they did. Lisa's advice: "Don't believe this. Check with the proper state officials. In many cases changes are permitted."

Her position is verified by Bret Lowell. He sees more negotiating on contract points going on now. He has found that "a prospective franchisee can negotiate more with a brand-new franchisor." He also notes that a franchisee who is considered "a big player"—i.e., someone who is going to buy multiple units or a large region—will have some clout and be able to negotiate more points. "However," Lowell is quick to point out, "there is a limit as to how far the franchise system will bend. They won't allow you to change things that challenge uniformity or economies of scale, for example. They say if we do it for you, we'll have to do it for everyone. Call it the grapevine effect."

Tip

Most major points of the franchise agreement will not be negotiated by the franchisor, so if there's something you cannot live with, be ready to walk away from the deal.

Franchisees need to realize that they're not getting involved in a one-to-one relationship, says Bret Lowell. Franchisors strive to keep everything uniform and shy away from making exceptions. The reasoning behind this is easy to understand. An exception for one franchisee can set a precedent for the entire system. This factor, however, should not keep you from requesting changes, but it should help you to set priorities and to negotiate only for those points that make or break the deal for you.

Franchise Fees and Royalties

Just about all franchisors require the franchisee to pay a franchise fee. It is the payment for admission and training in the franchisor's organized business system. The fee may be required in one lump sum or in installments and can range from a low of about $3000 to over $100,000. The majority of the franchisees interviewed paid in the $10,000 to $30,000 range, but, since many of them paid the fee three to five years ago, the average now is probably higher. If you are buying a large territory or region, you can expect a franchise fee that exceeds $100,000.

Tip

Be very sure you've settled on the right franchise, because once you have paid the fee it's doubtful you will get it back if you change your mind. Most fees are nonrefundable.

Trap

Don't be enticed by a franchisor's very low fee. Find out what it covers. If training, support, and marketing aren't included in the initial fee, you can end up paying much more on a piecemeal basis than you would with a higher fee that includes all these things.

In addition to an initial franchise fee, there is generally a continuing regular fee called a *royalty*. This is usually payable monthly or weekly and based on a percentage of gross sales. This payment covers the use of a trademark and tradename as well as continuing services, which include training programs, marketing and sales materials, construction and start-up assistance, site selection, new product development, newsletters, and regional and national meetings.

Tip

Be very careful with royalty fees that are paid on a weekly basis. Work this through in your cashflow projections. You don't want to be in the position of having to pay the franchisor when you have uncollected funds.

Royalty fees vary widely by franchisor and by industry. In our own survey, we found that nearly half of the franchisees paid 5 to 6 percent of their gross sales to the franchisor. But perhaps more interesting, about 8 percent of the franchisees paid no royalty at all and about 12 percent paid 10 percent or more in royalty.

The franchisees who did not pay a royalty were, for the most part, in businesses where the franchisee bought ongoing services and products from the franchisor. Some such businesses include Leadership Management (franchisee buys programming materials), Money Mailer (printing services from franchisor), and Citizens Against Crime (franchisor provides products for sale).

To be sure, in many systems a franchisee must buy products and services from the franchisor and still pay a royalty fee. In the case of a franchise with no royalty fee, a royalty can be captured in the obligatory product or service price.

Then, we have franchise systems requiring hefty fees of 10 percent or better. If your chosen franchise is in this category, find out *exactly* what you are getting for your money. We found these higher royalty fees in all types of businesses. The best course of action is to compare the franchisor's royalty fee to other franchise systems in the same sector. If other franchisors (in a similar business) are not charging an equivalent fee, then the management of the higher-priced franchise should give you some very specific reasons for its higher royalty.

Tip

Ask yourself this question when considering a royalty fee (especially one that seems high in comparison to other franchisors): Does the franchise have such *powerful* name recognition that the high royalty is warranted?

The only other variant you may find with royalty payments is that some are paid on a sliding scale. Usually these start at a number like 5 or 6 percent and can rise as high as 15 percent as gross sales increase. In these instances, you will need to do some careful calculations to make sure that the profit from increasing sales doesn't all end up going to the franchisor in royalty payments instead of to your bottom line.

Tip

Find out if franchisees are paying their royalties. It spells trouble if they aren't. Either they're not doing well enough to pay the fee or they're not satisfied with the franchisor's support and service.

Advertising Fees

The new UFOC guidelines require extensive disclosures regarding advertising funds. Careful reading of these disclosures and a discussion of any questionable points with franchise management should answer all your questions about what you will receive in exchange for the advertising fees.

Advertising fees, like royalty fees, vary from franchisor to franchisor and industry to industry. The fee can be a percentage of your gross sales or a flat fee paid on a monthly basis. In our survey, we found that although the majority of franchisees paid 1 to 3 percent of their gross sales in advertising fees, more than a quarter of them (29 percent) did not pay anything to the franchisor for advertising. Almost all the franchisors that did not levy advertising fees were in the start-up phase or were young franchise systems where a national advertising program hadn't yet been established. The franchisors did do local advertising but had not set up a fee for this support.

Tip

National advertising cannot be effective for a franchise system unless a critical mass of franchisees is located throughout the United States. If the system has few units and they are widely scattered, only local advertising will be cost-effective.

Many franchisors of a certain size, say, with 500 operating units or more, divide the advertising fee into two parts. One part is for a systemwide advertising fee, and the second is used for local or regional advertising through an advertising cooperative formed with other franchisees within the region.

Some questions that you should ask the franchisor about its advertising include:

1. How much of the fee is spent for national advertising? How will the fee be spent?

2. Is any of the advertising fee used for administrative purposes? If so, how much?

3. Are audited figures on advertising expenditures available to franchisees?

4. Are advertising materials, such as camera-ready art, circulars, direct-mail pieces, and posters provided to franchisees? Is there a cost?

5. Is there any input from franchisees on the use of advertising dollars?

We did hear quite a few complaints from our surveyed franchisees about the various advertising funds. Often, franchisees were unsure of how the funds were being used and didn't feel the advertising impact was sufficient for the money. However, the fast-food franchisees associated with renowned systems such as Wendy's and Pizza Hut were pleased with the advertising campaigns. These franchisees noticed a huge surge in business each time a new, national advertising campaign appeared.

Franchisor Training and Support

Virtually every franchise system offers a training program to new franchisees. This is vital because there's a good chance that the franchisee will be new to the industry. Only about a quarter of the franchise systems require previous experience in the industry. These are predominantly in businesses which require a very specialized knowledge or skill, for example, optical products and services, accounting and tax services, real estate services, and some restaurant systems. In any case, getting trained in the particulars of the franchisor's system is essential.

The franchise agreement should spell out all initial and continuing training obligations of the franchisor in detail. You should also query the franchisor about the following:

1. Is previous or related experience necessary to operate the franchise?

2. Is training optional, recommended, or mandatory?

3. What is the nature and extent of the training?

4. What are the costs, and who is responsible for paying? Do these costs include classroom training, lodging, meals, and transportation?

5. Where is the location of the training facilities?

6. Is the training of employees included in any training cost charge?

7. Will there be a continuing training program?

8. Will there be video or audio tapes or mailed written materials? Is there a charge?

9. Is start-up assistance provided by the franchisor? Is assistance from franchisor personnel provided for preopening and for a time after opening?

Tip

If the franchisor allows it, sit in on a training session *before* you buy the franchise.

What to Expect from Training

In our survey of franchisees, all said they had attended a training program of one kind or another. Training ranged in time from 2 to 3 days all the way up to 8 weeks or more. The longer stints were associated with those businesses that require a specialized skill or technical training or one of the very standardized fast food operations. The average training time was one to two weeks. More than 50 percent of the franchisees said that the training had been changed and extended since they bought the franchise. They also said they and others at the training session had complained to the franchisor that the time was too short to learn everything they had to know. So apparently franchisors are listening to complaints and suggestions of their franchisees and acting on them.

For example, Larry Gambino, a Priority Management franchisee (management skills program) was trained over four years ago in company headquarters in Vancouver, B.C. He recalls that it was adequate then but says the training program is now much improved. He also benefits from the new ongoing training, which is led by regional coaches. They meet with franchisees once a month to help keep them on track and maintain a focus on building the business.

Tip

Ken Dykhuis, a Mighty Distributing Co. franchisee (auto parts distribution), spent two weeks in the Atlanta corporate headquarters for training. When asked if the training was sufficient, Ken said, "You can always use more training but at some point you just have to go out and do it."

The majority of franchisors include the cost of training for the purchaser, the spouse, and usually one or two employees in the initial fee. There's less consensus regarding room, board, and transportation, but in general our surveyed franchisees paid these expenses out of their pockets.

The classroom training sessions are usually held at the corporate headquarters. Most franchisees agreed that they could have used more training in administration and especially in the computer systems. In addition to the classroom sessions, many of the franchisees also got on-the-job training held at corporate-owned units or other franchisee units. This experience was followed by onsite training and support, with most systems sending one or two company representatives to help franchisees through the early stages of their openings.

Jeff Grayson is a Pizzeria Uno (restaurant) franchisee who had lots of prior experience in the restaurant business. Even so, Grayson says, "I trained up in Framingham, Massachusetts, for 8 weeks, and it was well worth it. You're responsible for 50 to 100 employees per restaurant, so you better know the business." Then the franchisor sent a team of six people to help in opening the restaurant and to do things like going over menus with new employees. Jeff says, "The first restaurant opening is very tough, but subsequent stores are easier because then you can mix in some experienced employees with the new ones."

Buying into a new franchise system is likely to be a totally different experience. Ken Wisotzky was the first My Favorite Muffin (retail muffins) franchisee, with only one company store opened. There was no formal training program set up, so Ken got his training by working at the company store for a little over a week. The major problem, according to Wisotzky, was "that it seemed like a very easy operation," but he didn't realize then that the store had a relatively low-volume business. When he opened his own business, he found that he had more than double the number of customers. This meant he immediately needed additional employees and he also had to change some operational techniques to compensate for the greater volume of business.

On the positive end, the training program can pay some unexpected dividends. Take the experience of George Colgate, a VR Business Brokers (sales of small businesses) franchisee. Colgate trained for two weeks in the training center in Dallas. The first week he learned about business brokerage, and the second week concentrated on office management. As part of the training, new franchisees are put out on the street and have to make a cold call to see how it feels. This experience actually got George's business off to a great start. During training, he managed to list a business and sell a business.

A Structured Training Program

Let's look, for example, at how a very large franchisor of residential and commercial cleaning services, ServiceMaster, organizes its training program. The program is divided into two parts. First, there is the "production on-the-job training" where new franchisees spend two weeks with their distributor or qualified representatives, learning the fundamentals of the business. Next, there is a week-long session of concentrated training, called the "Academy." Franchisees then have up until the first 6 months of offering ServiceMaster services to the public to take and pass a written examination. The cost of the Academy is included in the initial franchise fee—as is the transportation, room, and board for one franchisee.

The Quality of Franchisor Support

Except in the case of franchise systems in transition (new ownership), all the interviewed franchisees believed they were receiving adequate or good support from the franchisor. As might be expected, franchisees often cited areas for improvement, but, surprisingly, most franchisees were pleased with franchisor support. Some franchisees were impressed, for example, that the system responds quickly to questions and does some hand-holding when necessary. They appreciated simple gestures such as having someone at the corporate office calling to offer support when they experienced a down day.

Most franchises offer a national convention for franchisees where ideas may be exchanged, franchisees can network, and the franchisor can communicate its plans for the future. Such conventions run the gamut from fairly simple working sessions to elaborate, gala affairs where the franchisor picks up all the expenses.

Franchisees with a Voice

A franchise advisory board made up of franchisees is fairly standard except for the start-up franchises. The quality of these boards varies. They may be rubber stamps of the franchisor philosophy or can be independent-thinking boards which really effect change.

The advisory board is probably the area most franchisees mentioned as needing improvement. Apparently this advisory group is, in most systems, just finding its way, and its effectiveness will improve as more and more franchisees voice their opinions.

When evaluating a franchise opportunity, look for systems where franchisees are encouraged to voice their opinions and to suggest improvements, rather than simply follow the rules. It is also critical that the franchisor have a support system in place which is able to respond not only to start-up problems but also to those encountered by the franchisee in the second, third, and subsequent years.

Term of Agreement, Renewal, and Termination

According to the International Franchise Association's "Franchising in the Economy 1989–1992," about 45 percent of the respondents to their survey in 1991 had 10-year franchise agreements. The second greatest number had 20-year agreements, followed by those with 5-year terms.

The term of the agreement is the number of years the franchisee may operate the business. When the term expires, the right and license to operate the business will end. Of course, many agreements provide for renewal rights, so that a franchisee has the option of extending the term of the contract.

Tip

Check the agreement carefully to see if the franchisor imposes a renewal fee. You may also be required to renew under the terms of the
franchisor's prevailing franchise agreement, leaving you open to the
possibility of higher royalties and advertising fees in the future.

Most of the franchisees we interviewed had five- to eight-year
contracts, a considerably shorter term than the respondents of the
IFA survey. Bret Lowell, a franchise attorney, noted that sometimes
franchisors impose even shorter terms so that they can "assess the
business on an ongoing basis." He says that, "Businesses change,
technologies change, and sometimes the original franchisee is no
longer right for the business. That's why many franchisors prefer to
go with 3 five-year term contracts instead of 1 fifteen-year term." On
a positive note, Lowell has found that most franchise contracts are
renewed.

An attorney can help you review the franchisor's provisions for renewal and termination. Determine, with your attorney, what specific
conditions must be met for renewal and the circumstances that
could lead to termination of the agreement before its expiration.

Tip

Engage a franchise attorney to look over your franchise opportunity
and participate in negotiations with the franchisor. About 70 percent
of the interviewed franchisees hired an attorney, but nearly everyone
commented that a specialized franchise attorney is the best choice.
One franchisee said she didn't want to hire a general attorney who
she'd be paying to learn about the franchise business.

You'll also want to consider and evaluate the franchisor's termination processes. Some of the questions you need answered are:

- What are the defaults for which there may be a termination?
- Are you given notice of a default and a reasonable amount of time
  to remedy it?

- Does the franchisor have any option to cancel the agreement other than for "good cause"?

- Under what conditions (if any) is the franchisee able to cancel the agreement?

- If the franchisee is not renewed or terminated, does the franchisor have a responsibility to buy back any equipment, inventory, or other assets?

- If there is an obligation to buy back franchisee assets, what are the purchase terms? Is there an independent appraisal?

- Does the franchisor have the right to take over your lease?

Trap

Check the agreement carefully for high sales quotas or high minimum inventory purchases. Not meeting these goals could result in termination of the franchise agreement.

The franchise agreement may also include a noncompete clause in the termination section. This clause will prevent a franchisee from competing in the same business for a period of years if the franchise business is terminated. Try to negotiate an agreement which excludes a noncompete covenant. As an example, a franchisee we interviewed in the photography business chose a franchise with a standard five-year noncompete clause. However, since the franchisee's entire business background had been in photography, he couldn't accept this condition. His attorney managed to have this clause deleted. If the franchisor won't budge on this point, you must carefully assess the risks and costs you will face if the franchise fails and you must leave the industry.

Exclusive Rights to Territories and Areas

Surprisingly, most of the franchisees interviewed had very loose arrangements, if any at all, regarding territorial rights for their franchises. Many franchisees said their territorial rights were not spelled out, not in writing, but that they had come to a verbal agreement which they accepted in good faith. This is not a very secure arrangement from either a legal or financial standpoint.

The franchisor's reticence to spell out the territory and exclusive area rights of franchisees in the franchise agreement has caused widespread discontent amongst franchisees. Let's examine some of the common ways franchisors approach the question of territorial rights and see what you can do to prevent potential problems.

Tip

Here's a question to ask the franchisor: "What guarantees do I have that a company-owned outlet or a new franchisee will not encroach on my marketing area?"

Defining Exclusivity

Depending on the business, there are all kinds of ways to define a territory. Sometimes, areas are defined by population ratios. For instance, one business services franchisee says there are no exclusive territories in his system and finds that it causes problems. A franchise is assigned for each 250,000 population. Consequently many franchisees service metro areas and can end up overlapping and competing with one another.

In other cases, the franchisee may be assigned specific accounts. Here the boundaries are a little clearer except that, in some instances, one franchisee can go into another franchisee's territory to sell a large account, if the decision maker is based in the first franchisee's territory.

Zip codes are yet another way that territories can be defined. Decorating Den, for instance, uses boundaries defined by zip codes. When a customer calls into the main office, however, from an area which is not in an assigned zip code, those calls are given to franchisees on a rotating basis. Pressed 4 Time franchise is another system which is governed by zip codes; 30,000 prime clients is considered a territory.

Protected Territories

The "protected territory" approach is a little more nebulous and is rarely written into the agreement. It is usually little more than an unwritten understanding between the franchisor and franchisee. Here are some typical franchisee situations:

■ A photo store owner initially had a 3-mile radius that was exclusive to his store. Now the radius around newer units has become smaller, and some stores are competing for the same business.

■ Another retail franchisee has an unwritten 3-mile radius rule between stores that has already been breached by the franchisor.

■ Sometimes, territories are clearly stipulated and enforced. For example, Lisa Brumm, a Formals Etc franchisee, has an exclusive territory spanning 25 miles. If any other franchisee wants to open shop there, it would have to pay Lisa and her mother a royalty. Also, their agreement allows for a larger "protected territory" where they have "first right of refusal" should a store open up.

Trap

Oral representations rarely hold up in court. If it's important to you, get it in writing.

Sometimes territorial rights carry with them certain obligations, especially if you are buying into a fairly large area. For example, Jeff Grayson, a Pizzeria Uno franchisee, has territorial rights to a large area around Orlando, Florida. In return for those rights he has to open a certain number of restaurants in a limited period. And if Arny Grushkin, a Unishippers franchisee with an exclusive territory, does not uphold the performance standards in his franchise agreement then Unishippers can buy back his franchise.

Selecting a Site

Site selection, as we have said earlier, can be critically important to the success of the franchise, especially one with heavy customer traffic. If the site or location of the business is important, the franchisor should help to select the site. At the least the franchisor should have criteria and guidelines to assist you in your site selection. Some of the guidelines used for selection are: trade area population, demographics, traffic patterns, competition, industry and office space, and visibility of signage. Often the franchisor has already identified and purchased a real estate site and then starts looking for the franchisee.

If the franchise management does not offer you advice or show a great deal of expertise in site selection—*beware!* After all, part of what you're paying for is the franchisor's experience at determining what will be a successful site. The franchisor should have a proven location standard to assist you.

Tip

If you are considering an urban location for your business, factor the following costs into your decision making: You will need to secure a business license, adhere to zoning requirements, and probably use union workers for any building improvements. Also, consider the increased expense of insurance and security.

Some questions to ask are:

1. Who finds the site? Who negotiates the lease or purchases/builds the facility?

2. If the franchisor has already picked out a site, how was its suitability determined?

3. Will the franchisor obtain and "build out" a site and then sublease it to you? What are the terms?

4. If the franchisee is to develop the site, are the plans and specifications provided? Does the initial fee cover this cost?

Are There Quotas?

Check the agreement to see if you must generate a specific volume to maintain an exclusive territory or to avoid termination. If the agreement has quotas, find out how realistic the numbers are. Talk to other franchisees and find out if the numbers are feasible.

We found that quotas are pretty rare; only one of the franchisees we interviewed had to meet a yearly sales quota. That franchisee, in a specialized personnel business, said that if he doesn't make the sales numbers, he has to compensate for the difference. The quotas increase each succeeding year, but he found that the quota numbers were quite reasonable.

Consequences of New Corporate Ownership

A change in franchise ownership can be good or bad for franchisees. A new owner can bring in additional resources, maybe a bigger customer base or better financing for the franchisees. Or a new owner can bring increased franchise fees or inflated prices of supplies and products in order to finance the purchase. Also, the new management might be inexperienced and execute bad decisions.

The change in management can be disruptive, particularly when the executive office has a revolving door. The owner of a business brokerage business was able to survive six changes of system ownership by "keeping his focus on selling businesses" despite the chaos. In another instance, after watching the franchise owners going public and then going private several times, the franchisees formed a separate franchisee organization in self-defense. Finally, lacking confidence in the leadership of each succeeding franchisor group, many of the franchisees stopped paying royalties, dropped the logo, and started conducting business independently.

In another corporate changeover example, a retail snack food franchisee was successful and happy for several years with the original franchise owners. When the originators of the concept sold out to a large conglomerate, everything changed. The franchisee says, "They now had a bunch of people who knew how to spend money (franchisees, for example, were flown out to corporate headquarters and were wined and dined) but lost touch with the basics." In addition, the system turned out vast quantities of product, but the product quality declined, and the franchise system could not support the huge amount of product. This meant the franchisees had to continually run specials to move the product. Eventually the conglomerate gave up on the franchise, and a succession of owners has followed. Now our franchisee is giving up on the franchise.

What can a franchisee do, if anything, to avoid the potential problem of changing ownership? Our unhappy franchisee above says, "In retrospect I would have tried to incorporate into the franchise agreement that if the company is sold or changed, I would have the option to get out of the contract."

From a franchise attorney's viewpoint, Bret Lowell tells us, "Assume when you buy the franchise that the management will change—sometimes for the best, but sometimes for the worst." He points out that even mature companies change, and in all companies an evolutionary process takes hold.

From a legal standpoint, you can do little to prevent a franchise company from being sold. Certainly, look at the age and goals of the owners when you investigate the franchise. Also find out how dedicated they are to the industry. This should give you some indication as to whether a corporate change might be imminent. But there are no guarantees, so this question of corporate change-over remains one of the areas of risk when you buy a franchise.

Buying a Previously Owned Franchise

Let's suppose you are interested in buying a resale franchise. You will be purchasing the franchise from the present franchisee, but you will still have to sign an agreement with the franchisor. Besides the agreed-upon purchase price with the franchisee, often you will be asked to pay a transfer fee to the franchise system. In the case of one franchisee we talked to, it was one-third the current franchise fee.

The price of a resale franchise is usually higher than a new franchise bought from the franchisor because you will be buying a customer base, equipment, and the goodwill of an operating business. How then do you determine if the franchise is priced fairly? We asked George Colgate at VR Business Brokers how a prospective buyer should evaluate the value of a resale franchise. Colgate says that often ongoing businesses are priced according to this formula: One year's net profit, plus inventory value, plus fixtures and equipment value, plus real estate value (if applicable), plus goodwill. The dollar amount assigned to goodwill can sometimes be a sticking point. Goodwill is an abstract factor that can be defined as the favor or prestige that a business has acquired beyond the mere value of what it sells.

Colgate also suggests that the buyer should analyze the cashflow of the business by studying the owner's financial records. The prospective buyer should determine if the following three goals can be met:

1. An 8 to 12 percent (for today's market) return on investment on the downpayment and start-up capital. (The reasoning here is that you could be receiving interest on the monies invested in the business so you would expect at least a conservative return on your investment money.)
2. The throw-off of enough cash to service the debt and eventually retire it.
3. A payment of a reasonable wage to the owner-operator.

Tip

You may have to arrange a different type of training program with the franchisor if you buy a resale franchise. A case in point is Mike Bueti, a Merry Maids (residential cleaning) franchisee. He found that the one week's training provided by the franchisor was not sufficient because he had inherited 19 employees and established accounts through the resale. He didn't have the option of learning as he went along as most franchisees do as they build the business. Bueti had to hit the ground running to keep the ongoing business running smoothly.

Buying a previously owned franchise is becoming a viable option for more and more investors. Assuming the business is reasonably successful, here are some of the reasons for the increasing popularity of this choice:

- *Faster profits and owner's draw.* Since there are no real start-up costs and the business is ongoing, you should see a profit and draw a salary almost immediately.

- *Simplified planning.* Projections are easier to make because you have historical records as a basis for financial and marketing forecasting.

- *Expedited financing.* Often the previous owner will accept a downpayment and then a monthly payment until the agreed upon price is covered. The new owner will not have to seek financing from lending institutions and private investors.

- *Built-in advantages.* The new owner usually inherits experienced employees, established suppliers, and loyal customers.

If you'd like to explore the idea of buying a previously owned business, you have to know where to look to find them. Here are four suggestions:

1. If you're settled on a particular franchise, talk to other franchisees. They often know about resales in the system.
2. Talk to the franchisor.
3. Look for advertisements in local and national newspapers.
4. Find a business broker specialized in franchises. These brokers are paid by percentage commissions on the completed sales. Commissions are usually paid by the seller of the business.

As you may have guessed, not all resales are good deals. Look out for resales where antiquated facilities and inventory are calculated into the purchase price. You may have to add additional monies to modernize the facilities and replace the inventory. The biggest problem, though, may be encountered if you buy a franchise which has been allowed to deteriorate. You may be inheriting the ill will of the customers, and retrieving alienated customers will be very difficult.

Tip

Here's some good advice from Jeanette Fuller, who bought a Tutor Time Learning Center resale with her husband. She says, "If you are buying a resale—especially one that is in difficulty—*negotiate* so that the franchisor will be obliged to buy back the franchise if it is not successful in a certain amount of time."

Selling your Business

The ability to sell or transfer your franchised business is an important part of the franchise agreement. Check the franchise agreement to see what the franchisor stipulations are for resales. You should also check to see that the franchise is assignable or that it may be sold if you die or are disabled.

Franchisors have a big interest in knowing who will be buying your business, because they will expect the sales level to be maintained and they will want to know that the owner can pay the royalties and other fees. In most cases franchisees must ask the franchisor for approval of a transfer. In practice, most resales that make sense will not be held up by the franchisor. No one wants to keep an unhappy franchisee.

Final Words

By the time you're thinking about signing a franchise agreement there should be little left to investigate and no real surprises. If, however, you find yourself uneasy and strongly opposed to several stipulations of the agreement, get ready to move on to another opportunity.

6

Finding the Best
Sources for Financing
Your Business

*How difficult was it to finance the
business? Very difficult. And we had fairly
liquid assets (stocks and bonds) to use for
collateral and an excellent credit record.*

MARCY PINNELL
*Wee-bag-it (food take-out and
delivery) franchisee*

Many franchisees answered our questions about financing with a
groan. In most cases, piecing together the financial package is a
challenging but not impossible task. The majority of franchisees do
not receive all their funding from one source. Rather, they use a
combination of sources to finance their businesses. First they see
how much they can contribute from their personal savings. Then,
roughly in the order of popularity, they turn to family or other investors, franchise system financing, bank loans, government programs,
a note to the previous owner in the case of a resale, lines of credit,
home equity loans, limited partnerships, and venture capital. A discussion of these sources as well as a few more ideas in this chapter

should start you off on the right track to getting your chosen business financed.

Before you begin to try to raise the necessary capital, you need to take a realistic look at the financial burdens. No matter how great a business person you are, chances are slim that you can put together a financial package for a major fast-food franchise that requires an investment of $750,000 or more if you have little or no collateral. Actually, it is doubtful that you will even get this far, because the lack of collateral will show up on the franchisor's qualifying questionnaire and the process will come to a halt.

Choosing a Source of Capital

If you can finance the business entirely from your own personal funds and savings, congratulations, you can skip this section. If that is not the case, read on and engineer your plan of action.

Maybe you have a good portion of the money needed, maybe a fair amount, or maybe none at all. The shortfall—the money that you don't have to pay the franchise fees, to cover the start-up costs, and to fund daily operations—must be borrowed or raised.

Using Debt

If you borrow the money, you are using debt financing. You will probably borrow from one or a combination of the following: commercial banks, government-sponsored bank loans, franchise system loans, home-equity loans, and credit card loans. Then, too, if your franchise is a resale, you may arrange a payment plan with the previous owner, whereby you pay a set amount each month to buy the business on installment.

Tip

Keep in mind two points, whatever the source of your debt financing. First, securing a loan takes a great deal of time, even if you have an impeccable credit history. Second, there is often more cost to borrowing money than the interest alone. Many of the lending institutions charge points on the front end for an approved loan. For example, a $20,000 loan can result in a front-end charge of $500 to $2000, depending on your geographic location.

Using Equity

Although debt financing is far more prevalent for franchise investments, equity financing is another way to raise money. The big difference between the two is that in debt financing you will have an obligation to pay the borrowed sum but you will retain control of the business; in equity financing, however, you are giving up a part of the business to an investor or investors in exchange for their financing. The investors will claim some control of the business operations, they will own some of the assets, and they will share some earnings. You will not have a set debt obligation to repay as you would with a monthly loan payment to a bank, for example. The investor will be taking a risk as to when and how much of the investment he or she will recoup as well as whether there will be a return on the investment.

Family and Friends

One of the most common ways of using equity financing is through investing by family and friends. They are often the first sources of financing that come to mind for many franchisees. After all, family and friends know your capabilities, and they want to help you succeed. As investors, they will, no doubt, want to have some input into how the business is run and be regularly apprised as to the progress of the venture. These demands are perfectly consistent with the role of equity investors.

The threat of problems and discord, however, looms larger when the family or friend investors are directly involved in the operation of the business. To be sure, some of these set-ups work very well, with everyone pulling for a common goal. However, it is more probable that you, as an owner-manager, will have to resolve conflicts between what is good for the franchise and what family or friends think is good for them. In general, you can anticipate more stress in a family-owned business, even if you are the largest stockholder. You will have to be tactful and patient with the family investors. When several family members invest in a business, the conflict often revolves around defining priorities—the business or the family.

Tip

Carefully consider how you will organize and operate the business to minimize potential problems if your business is financed by family or friends.

Partnerships

Another financial route is to take a partner. In a partnership you will share the equity of the business with another person. Such a relationship can develop by simply discussing your franchise opportunity with a friend or acquaintance and deciding to go into business together. The partnership may be established by oral or written agreement. However, I strongly encourage you to engage an attorney to formulate a written agreement that details the partners' rights and obligations.

The most important thing to remember in any partnership arrangement is that the relationship must be based on trust and confidence. Your capital and your personal assets can be put on the line by a partner's actions. Whether your business thrives or fails will depend largely on your choice of a partner.

Venture Capital

Another way to raise capital using business equity is to team up with a venture capital firm. Although some franchisees have received venture capital support, most venture capital firms would not even consider funding a single-location franchise. They are generally chasing the big deal where the capital requirements are in the million-dollar range and where the business can generate a very high return on investment. If you are considering a multiunit franchise deal, a large territory agreement, or a high-cost investment such as a hotel or motel franchise, contacting venture capital firms should be at the top of your list.

Limited Partnership

Setting up a limited partnership is another way to sell equity in the business. The application of this method, though, has very limited use for franchisees. Limited partnerships are usually relegated to specific industries, most often the restaurant business and real estate developments. This type of partnership gives investors special tax advantages and the advantage of limited liability. If the business fails, limited partners can lose only their original investment, any additional capital contribution, and their portion of the assets of the firm. General partners, however, have unlimited liability as in any ordinary partnership.

The general partner is the person putting together the deal—the franchisee—usually someone who has managerial expertise and experience in the industry. The limited partners are simply investors who will have little or nothing to say about the operation of the business but who expect to have their investment plus a nice return paid to them for the use of their capital.

Leasing

You might include a leasing arrangement in your financial planning. This doesn't quite fall under either traditional debt or equity financing. Often leasing is part of the package called "franchisor-sponsored financing," and it entails paying a monthly fee to rent equipment, furnishings, and fixtures from the franchisor. Usually there is a buy-out amount at the end of the leasing period, where you have the option of buying the leased equipment or furnishings.

Leasing can be a very attractive option. Although you will pay a greater net amount for the leased equipment, it eliminates the need of coming up with the full amount to purchase the equipment for start-up. Also, in many industries the equipment will be obsolete in 5 or 10 years, so when your leasing arrangement terminates you can sign another lease for the newest models.

In addition to franchisor-sponsored leasing, commercial leasing companies write leases on everything from computers to copiers, machinery, fixtures, and vehicles. Most leases are for the long term, maybe 10 years, and require the lessee to pay all the expenses related to maintenance, insurance, and taxes during the lease's term. Leasing often requires collateral from the lessee—such as the pledging of assets and personal guarantees.

First Things First: A Basic Business Plan

Whether you are going to finance your business by using debt or by using equity or by combining the two, the first step is to prepare a business plan. If you've done one before, you're ahead of the game. If not, I suggest you ask your accountant to help you prepare the financial parts of the business plan. Or, you could see if the franchisor offers assistance to prospective franchisees in putting together a business plan (and a loan-proposal package). Several software packages and books on the market can take you through a viable business plan format step by step.

The purpose of the business plan is to tell would-be lenders and investors what the business is, why it's a sound investment, how the business will be operated, when you expect it to be profitable, and how you will pay back the loan or the investment.

Your starting point is the Uniform Franchise Offering Circular (UFOC). The UFOC is a detailed investment prospectus provided by the franchisor and will contain much of the information you'll need to include in your business plan. In addition, since the fortunes of franchisor and franchisee are often intertwined, the lender or investor will want to know about the franchise system as well as about how you will conduct the business.

A Basic Business Plan Guide

As a guide, the following is a rundown of the format and information most business plans will contain. (Note: A sample business plan format appears at the end of this chapter.)

After a cover page, giving your name (or company name), address, telephone number, the name of the business, and the name of the individual or company to whom the plan is being submitted, you will normally include a table of contents. Then we get to the body of the plan.

Summary. Often called an "executive summary," this is maybe the most important part of your plan in terms of potential results. It gives lending officers, investors, and potential partners their first (and perhaps only) impression of your venture. These people have many demands on their time, and you can't rely on them to sit down, put up their feet, and casually read through your business proposal. Instead, your executive summary will have to hook them right from the beginning and get them interested in knowing more about you and your proposed business. Otherwise your proposal can land at the bottom of the pile without even a cursory review.

The summary—no longer than 1 or 2 pages—should describe the proposed franchise business with some detailing of the products or services that the franchise will sell. Next, write a brief overview of its industry, and, if possible, include some industry statistics and forecasts.

Follow up that overview with a profile of the franchise. Think about the characteristics that first sold you on it and emphasize those points in the summary. Also, include basic background information such as the number of years in the business, number of franchise outlets, and geographic range of operating franchises. Conclude with any thing else that makes the franchisor positively stand out.

Finally, you must state the amount of the loan request, or the amount of investment money needed. Along with this goes the intended use of the capital requested, for example, building costs, working capital, inventory, and equipment. Then the sentence the reader is looking for: how and when you will repay the loan or the investment.

Tip

Ask someone whose opinion you respect to read the executive summary before you submit it. Ask that person to flag both those things that capture interest and those that put the business in a negative light. Revise your summary if necessary.

Management. In the mind of the lender or the investor, the quality of the management team is of utmost importance. They will carefully scrutinize management credentials. Bear in mind that because your business is a franchise, potential lenders and investors will also evaluate the quality of the management of the franchise system.

You need to point out how the chief executive officer and other key managers of your business are uniquely qualified to make the franchise a success. Back up these assertions with professional résumés. Remember that you're trying to make the reader feel confident about your abilities to operate the new business successfully.

If you are applying for a bank loan or a government-backed loan, you will need to include your personal financial statement (and that of any other person or persons listed as principal owners). You should already have this information on hand, since you probably submitted it to the franchisor as a first step in the qualifying process.

Business Description.   You must choose whether your business will be operated as a sole proprietorship, a partnership, or a corporation. Although a sole proprietorship is the simplest and least expensive way to operate a business, it is normally prudent to incorporate so that the company's liabilities are separate from your own.

The content will vary depending on the business formation selected. If you will do business as a corporation, include the names and addresses of the shareholders, directors, and officers. If the business is a partnership, include the names and addresses of each partner. (The pros and cons of the various legal business formations are discussed in Chapter 7.)

Elaborating on information already in the summary, provide a description of the industry and your particular products or services. Include information such as the current dollar volume of the industry and the volume forecast for the next five years. Emphasize the market potential and the upward trend for the industry's products or services. For the most part, this information can be taken directly from the UFOC. You may also include pictures of products, retail locations, or anything else to help the lender or investor to better understand your business.

Marketing Plan.   After you've described the business in somewhat general terms, then it's time to get into specific details. You need to walk the reader through a point-by-point plan of how you will market and sell the product or service in your particular location or territory.

Tip

Don't confuse marketing with sales. Sales are the result of a well-thought-out marketing plan.

Your business or service is not for everyone, so you will have to identify the characteristics of the people who will most likely buy your product or service. This is called "market segmentation." You will be dividing the mass market into smaller submarkets, each with unique buying characteristics. Choose the markets you intend to reach and give their characteristics in this section.

The franchisor should be able to help with the information by providing you with basic demographic information on its customer base. Identify potential customers in terms of age, sex, income level, geographic dispersion, educational level, and perhaps more explicit behavioral traits. You can integrate this information into your marketing plan, showing how your customer base has all the right characteristics.

Depending on the nature of your business, your description of the customer base can be general or highly specific. If you're opening a fast-food restaurant you might say it's the entire neighborhood. If you're opening a business service, you might be very specific and say, for instance, that your customers are purchasing managers in industrial plants.

If you have a strictly defined area or locality in which to do business, state what it is. Describe the rationale behind the site selection and show how you will operate a successful business in this locale.

An analysis of the *competition* in the defined marketplace is also in order. You'll have to do some homework here and find out what competing products and services are out there, how they're marketed, and what they cost. Analyze the competition and then look at your own products or services. You must come up with at least one competitive advantage that can be used against your major competition. For example, maybe the quality of your product is superior, maybe the services you provide are unique, or perhaps your products or services cost 10 percent less than the competition. Don't overlook seemingly minor points, such as longer store hours or a more attractive location, that can be developed into your competitive edge.

Next, describe how you will sell and promote your products or services. If the franchisor has a national advertising campaign to which you contribute, describe how these ad dollars are used and their expected impact on your business. Your local advertising and promotion plans will also be of interest to the reader. Indicate how your promotional money will be spent and for which media. Include innovative ideas that you have for reaching the greatest number of customers.

Financial Forecast.   Since you are just starting out, you will have no actual financial data, so your financial analysis will be "pro forma." *Pro forma* means that the data is hypothetical and not actual. And so the pro forma cashflow analysis will predict income and expenses in a future period, rather than actual performance in the past.

You can deluge the reader of your business plan with tons of financial materials, and, if you think it will help your case, go ahead and do it. However, you must include three types of financial statements: a pro forma balance sheet (also called "financial statement") beginning at start-up and on to the end of the second year, a two-year projected cashflow statement, and a two-year projected profit and loss statement.

If you need help formulating the cashflow and the profit and loss statements, refer to Chapter 4. The third statement in your package is the balance sheet. Figure 6-1 shows a sample balance sheet. The sample balance sheet shows your company's financial condition for the period just before opening. The second column is the financial state of the company at the end of year one, and the third column is the financial state at the end of year two.

Loan or Investment Request.   The balance sheets, cashflow information, and profit and loss statements culminate with a statement regarding your loan or investment needs. You must state this in precise terms and then tell the reader exactly how you will use these funds. In addition, you should indicate what your personal cash investment is, and you should spell out the terms you are requesting for either the loan or the investment.

		Balance sheet as at	
	Opening	End year one	End year two
Assets			
Cash	70,000	7,312	14,152
Accounts receivable		12,000	13,200
Inventory		11,250	12,375
Equipment		25,000	25,000
Less accumulated depreciation		5,000	10,000
	0	20,000	15,000
Franchise fee		25,000	25,000
Less accumulated amortization		5,000	10,000
	0	20,000	15,000
Total assets	70,000	70,562	69,727
Liabilities & owner's equity			
Note payable	40,000	37,204	34,408
Owner's capital			
Beginning capital	30,000	30,000	33,358
Net income		9,358	13,961
(Less withdrawals)		(6,000)	(12,000)
Ending capital	30,000	33,358	35,319
Total liabilities & owner's capital	70,000	70,562	69,727
SOURCE: Dan Lasman, Hampstead Partners Inc., Wilton, Connecticut.			

Figure 6-1. Sample Balance Sheet.

Other Documentation. Depending on the nature of your business, here is some supporting documentation you may want to include:

- A copy of your franchise agreement
- A copy of your real estate lease agreement
- A copy of a leasing agreement for equipment or furniture
- A list of the insurances you carry

Tip

When you complete your business plan, you will have a blueprint for your business. Besides the use of the business plan as a necessary money-raising tool, you will benefit personally from doing it. Writing a business plan forces you to think through all the various aspects of the business. You will find it useful to refer to the business plan periodically over the first hectic year or two to help keep on track and reinforce focus on your goals.

A Closer Look at Debt Financing

Since the majority of franchisees use debt franchising, at least in part, to finance their franchise choice, let's look at the most popular avenues a little more closely.

Do Banks Deliver?

Almost all the franchisees surveyed did not have very positive experiences in their quests for bank loans. Many banks have cut back (or are at an almost nonexistent level) on so-called risky loans to small businesses. Apparently, they are trying to retrench and to repair their own balance sheets as a result of the excesses of the 1980s.

In all cases, commercial banks are looking for an adequate amount of collateral to cover any loan they extend to you. However, the bank is not really interested in owning your house, your boat, or your business real-estate. The bank is looking for a certainty that you will repay the debt in full. And so, even with a pledge of your house and your own savings invested in the business, the bank may still turn you down.

Tip

Some business investments fare better with banks than others. If your business has hard assets—things like equipment, inventory, and real estate—which can be used as collateral, you will have a much better chance at bank funding than a service business with only accounts receivable to offer.

Many franchisees told stories of how their first stop for a business loan was a local commercial bank, where they were turned down.

The fact that the business was a franchise was of some help, since most bankers are aware of the high success statistics for franchises. But such awareness wasn't always enough to win a "yes."

Others have succeeded in securing bank loans. Marcie Pinnell, Wee-bag-it's first franchisee, managed to finance about 75 percent of the investment through her bank. She and her husband were somewhat surprised at the difficulty involved, considering they were using fairly liquid investments of stocks and bonds as collateral. They also made up a complete business plan with five-year cashflow projections for presentation to the bank. Their assessment: The franchise format was a plus (even though they were the first franchisee); their financial status and credit record was a plus; and the fact that the business was a restaurant was a negative. The bank looked at a restaurant as being a more risky investment than others, given the high failure rate of this type of business.

A Computertots franchisee, Ann Brown, had relatively modest financial needs, since her franchise is operated out of her home. She managed to cover half the investment with a loan from a relative and the other half from a bank. She, too, prepared a business plan but backed it up with some clever market research. She called all the day care centers in her area and obtained tentative agreements to sign on with her computer program from many of them. She was able to report all this to the bank, and they were impressed. Another plus for the bank was the fact that she was already working for another franchisee, so they felt she knew the business.

Tip

If you don't have enough confidence in the probable success of the franchise to pledge your own collateral, you should re-evaluate the franchise opportunity.

SBA Loan Guarantee Programs

After being rejected by several banks for a loan, most franchisees start thinking about securing a U.S. government Small Business Administration (SBA) loan. In fact, several of the franchisees we interviewed did just that. Unfortunately, the popular SBA loan-guarantee program has a limited budget and is prone to run out of money. Demand from small businesses for the government-guaranteed loans has been growing while the budget has not. The demand for the guarantees is likely to continue to outstrip the supply. Give this funding a try, but don't rely on it and certainly give yourself a back-up position.

Here's how the SBA-guaranteed loan program works. You still apply for a commercial bank loan. If the bank rejects your application for a loan on the basis of your financial profile, you become eligible to apply for an SBA-guaranteed loan. The bank you applied to may be part of the SBA-backed loan programs and, if so, will encourage you to reapply through this program. Otherwise, once a bank has rejected your loan request, you may initiate the contact with SBA yourself.

About 500 lenders, both commercial banks and nonbank lenders, participate in the SBA certification program. However, a lender does not have to be part of the certification program to submit an application. It could take more time to complete the process, though, since the SBA gives special status to certified lenders. In addition, the SBA loan application is quite lengthy and could present a problem to someone unfamiliar with this type of document. An experienced SBA lender often will help with the paperwork or do it entirely, for a fee.

If you qualify for the SBA loan guarantee program, the government guarantees the loan for up to 90 percent of the value (current average is about 81 percent). Your loan application still goes to the lender (the bank) for initial review, and it, in turn, forwards the application and the credit analysis to the nearest SBA office. The program requires that the borrower pledge some form of collateral. If the SBA approves, the lender closes the loan and disburses the funds.

The SBA program provides a good opportunity for the lender and the borrower alike. The banks are relieved, since a large percentage of the loan is guaranteed by the government, reducing their risk. The borrower, you, the franchisee, can get long repayment periods, often not available otherwise to small businesses, at a very favorable interest rate.

For a limited number of instances, the SBA will make a direct loan (not a guaranteed loan). Availability is restricted to franchisees in high unemployment areas who are unable to obtain guaranteed loans and to handicapped persons, Vietnam veterans, and disabled veterans. The number of these congressionally funded direct loans are even more limited than the SBA-guaranteed loans.

Here are the experiences of two franchisees who have used the SBA-backed loan program:

- Judy Gedman's accounting background helped her to put together a top-notch loan proposal package to fund her FastSigns franchise. The SBA loan was approved with a seven-year term payout and the usual pledging of collateral. It took three months to get approval and funding. Her biggest complaint is that the money was doled out by the bank. She was asked to submit expenditures on a case-by-case basis, even though the entire loan amount had been approved.

- Other franchisees have had more difficult experiences. The two owners of a retail store also went to the SBA after having major problems with the banks. However, says one of the owners, "the experience was a nightmare. We applied in August but only received the approval in December. There was an awful lot of paperwork. Every few weeks they would call up and ask for something new." At first the bank—with SBA approval—only paid for invoices as they were submitted, but, when the franchise owners strongly complained to the lending bank, the entire loan sum was released.

Tip

Qualifying for an SBA loan guarantee does not eliminate the need to put up your own personal collateral. The same assurances to the lender are still required, despite the government guarantee.

Other SBA-Related Loan Sources

The *Small Business Investment Companies* (*SBICs*) are independent venture capital groups licensed by the government to lend funds to small business start-ups. SBICs have access to SBA-guaranteed funds. Like most venture capital groups, SBICs often want an equity stake in the company and a managerial role. There is generally long-term loan financing in exchange for the equity position.

You'll find SBICs in most cities in the United States, some of which are bank affiliates or subsidiaries of other financial institutions. Some of the SBICs even specialize in working with franchisees. For a list of SBICs, call or write to the National Association of Small Business Investment Companies, 512 Washington Bldg., Washington, DC, 20005, (202)638-3411.

At recent franchise shows I saw several *Small Business Lending Companies*. Licensed by the SBA, these companies operate under the SBA 7-A Program. Long-term financing is available through these companies—if you qualify. Qualifications are generally the same as for commercial banks, but the loan rates will probably be better and the terms longer. Talk to a small business lending company representative when you visit a franchise show. Examples of these companies are The Money Store (Encino, California), PMC Capital, Inc. (Dallas, Texas), and Allied Capital Corp. (Washington, D.C.).

System Financing and Leasing

About 30 percent of the franchise systems have a program which aids the franchisee in financing the business and/or leasing the necessary facilities and equipment. Franchisors offer this service to make their franchises more attractive when the choice of a franchise is being made. Also, offering financing allows the franchisor to sign up people who fit their ideal franchisee criteria but are deficient in financial capabilities.

Sometimes the franchisor provides the financing, and other times the franchisor enlists a third party to provide the help. Here are some of the types of programs available:

- The Lemon Tree (unisex haircutting franchise) offers in-house financing up to one-half of the franchise fee and about one-half of the equipment costs (total amount around $10,000) to qualified franchisees.

- ServiceMaster franchises through its ServiceMaster Acceptance Co. Limited Partnership (SMAC), offers financing to franchisees who have passed its credit check. Up to 70 percent financing is available for the initial fee and the purchase of supplies and products. The interest rate is competitive and the loan term at this writing is five years.

- VR Business Brokers will finance a portion of the $24,000 initial fee. The franchisee must put $14,000 down and the company will carry a note for $10,000, payable over two years.

- Comet 1 Hr Cleaners & Laundry utilizes a third-party financer, as do many other franchise systems. Stephens Finance Corp., Little Rock, Arkansas (a popular financer for many systems) will finance up to 70 percent of the cost of equipment for five years for qualified franchisees.

Equipment Leasing

Since equipment often comprises 25 to 75 percent of the start-up costs, leasing the equipment can be a very effective way to cut down on your up-front cash needs. Leasing can be handled directly by the franchisor or by a leasing firm.

Subway, with about 7000 units, offers an in-house equipment leasing program. Subway buys the equipment and then leases it to the franchisee. The equipment lease runs for five years but carries a hefty interest rate. Likewise, a Fax 9 franchisee can finance the equipment needed through the system in a 36-month lease with a 10 percent buyout at the end of the lease.

Franchises with heavy equipment needs such as restaurants, lawn services, and hair salons often make arrangements with leasing firms if they are unable to offer their own leasing programs.

The franchisee will usually pay a rate about 2 to 3 percent higher than commercial banks when using these companies. However, since small business loans through commercial banks are sparse, the higher interest rate can be an acceptable tradeoff. Also, unlike traditional lenders' requirements for personal equity or collateral, the leasing firm uses the leased asset as collateral. The leasing firms often have a close relationship with the franchisor and sometimes require the franchisor to sign a repurchase agreement as additional security against default.

Creative System Approaches to Investing

In response to prospective franchisee's complaints about the problems of raising investment capital, franchisors are beginning to look for creative ways to lower the investment cost for franchisees. We hope this becomes a trend. The number of franchise systems that offer some kind of financial help for franchisees will, no doubt, be growing. But in the meantime we already have companies which are structuring their franchise offers in a way that can bring in a wider array of franchisees.

One of these is Interim Services, Inc., a $900 million company owned by H&R Block, with a health care subsidiary called Interim Healthcare. The company is in one of the fastest growing industries in the United States, home health care. Interim Healthcare places nurses, doctors, therapists, nurses aides, and home care workers in the patient's home.

The company says that in response to investors' requests for an arrangement which would give them more support from corporate headquarters but lower startup costs, it devised the Interim Healthcare licensing program. In the licensee relationship the investor pays $5000 up front and will eventually have a total investment of about $75,000 to $100,000 to cover startup and ongoing operational expenses. The gross profit of the company is split, with 75 percent going to the licensee and 25 percent to Interim Healthcare.

In the traditional Interim franchise option the amount of operating capital needed to start the business can be as high as $200,000, because franchisees must have the cash to take care of payroll, bookkeeping, and other overhead costs. However, there is no 25 percent "split" for the parent company.

In the licensee mode, the parent company performs specific services such as weekly payroll funding, payments for social security, federal, and state unemployment insurance and the like, plus invoicing clients, management reports, and monthly profit and loss statements. The program is designed as a complete turn-key system with the parent office performing the majority of "back-office" functions, albeit for a price.

Another franchise system which allows the business investor to pick a program which fits his or her financial situation is Jani-King, a commercial cleaning company. Carla Cunningham and her husband William own a Jani-King franchise in Philadelphia. Carla likes the way the program works because in the beginning it's quite possible for a husband and wife to work a regular job and do the commercial cleaning part-time.

The system works like this. The initial fee you pay depends upon what package is chosen. The franchisee can buy a package which guarantees accounts worth $1000 per month, $2000 per month, etc. If anything happens to an account, the franchisor will replace it.

If your business is working well and you want to go full-time or expand, you can add to your accounts by paying a "finders fee" of three times a monthly billing for a new account which the franchisor gives you. The franchisor, at least in the beginning, is your sales and marketing department.

The franchisee can also prospect for new accounts. The franchise system will send someone from the corporate office to help make a professional presentation to the potential customer.

Another program offered by a few systems utilizes an initial fee payment but no royalties. This is apparently in response to some franchisees' complaints about ongoing royalties. In the franchise systems that offer this, the franchisee will pay for corporate services on a needs basis, instead of paying an ongoing monthly royalty fee.

Homes and Credit Cards

There's no doubt that many franchisees rely on home equity loans or second mortgages to finance their new businesses. If you don't own your home or have sufficient equity in it, this option is not open to you. Several franchisees we interviewed went this route for financing. If putting your home on the line as collateral makes you very nervous, however, I would investigate other options first.

Tip

Stuart Ruben, a Money Mailer franchisee, recommends "using a home equity line of credit that you can draw on. But get the line before you buy the franchise—when you have an income coming in."

Several franchisees interviewed used lines of credit from credit card companies. Although no disasters were reported, this should be a last resort type of financing, since the interest rates are normally very high and you can be seduced into only paying minimal monthly amounts when cashflow is tight. In general, if you must use these credit lines, look for the lowest interest rates and draw on the lines only for small sums which you expect to repay quickly.

Final Words

If you are convinced (you've done *everything* we talked about in the preceding chapters) that your choice will result in a profitable business, go ahead and look at all these sources of financing. Combine two, three, or more sources in any way that makes sense for you.

Business Plan Guide

Cover Page

Name (your name or company name): _____

Address:_____

_____

Telephone: _____

Name of Business: _____

_____

Business Plan Submitted to: _____

Table of Contents

Summary   page___

Management   page ___

Business Description   page ___

Marketing Plan   page ___

Financial Forecast   page ___

Loan (or Investment) Request   page ___

Other Documentation   page ___

Summary
Brief statements of following: business description (products or services), overview of industry, franchise profile, amount of loan request or investment capital needed, intended use of the capital, and details on repayment of loan or investment capital.

Management
- Names, addresses, ages, education, and business experiences of CEO and other key personnel

(Continued)

- Personal financial statement of prospective franchisee and any other principal owners if applying for a bank or government-banked loan

- Names and experience of top franchisor management

Business Description

- Legal business form (sole proprietorship, partnership, or a corporation).

- For sole proprietorship: name of owner. For partnership: names and addresses of each partner. For corporation: names and addresses of the shareholders, directors, and officers.

- General information on industry and franchise.

Marketing Plan

- Customer base (demographics)
- Rationale for site selection
- Analysis of the competition
- Advertising and promotional plans

Financial Forecast

- Pro forma balance sheet
- Projected cashflow
- Projected profit and loss

Loan or Investment Request

State the amount of your loan or investment needs, use of the funds, and the terms you are requesting.

Other Documentation

Anything else which will help your case or help the reader understand the business.

7

Special Programs and Financing for Women, Minorities, and Veterans

There are lots of leasing programs
available to minorities, but they don't
really own the assets. We felt that
minorities had to build the kind of real
wealth that comes with owning land and a
restaurant.   WALT SIMON
on the KFC Minority
Franchise Program

In the past, women, minorities, and veterans were frequently at a disadvantage when it came to buying a business. Often, they were qualified in one respect but then lacked another element—collateral, net worth, or business experience—that traditional financial institutions require. Now franchising systems are welcoming these groups into the franchisee fold. Some franchise systems are leveling the playing field by providing special management and financial programs for these candidates. Those new incentives coupled with federal, state, and local government programs make investing in a franchise a real possibility for a more diverse group of people. This chapter will take a look at some of the opportunities earmarked for specific groups.

Help for Minorities

Nearly one of every four Americans is a member of the black, Hispanic, native American, or Asian ethnic communities. Some franchisors are responding to these numbers by setting up formal minority franchise recruitment programs. Others are at least showing increased sensitivity to the special needs of minority franchisees.

Those efforts are encouraged by the International Franchise Association (IFA), primarily a franchisor organization, which urges its membership to institute or enlarge minority recruitment programs. The IFA has formed alliances with such groups as the NAACP, U.S. Hispanic Chamber of Commerce, and the U.S. Commerce Department's Minority Business Development Agency. The IFA also serves as a clearinghouse for information on minority-oriented programs. For guidance and additional information, contact: Terrian Barnes-Bryant, vice president, Research/Minority and Women's Affairs, at (202)628-8000.

Some of the most impressive programs for minorities have been instituted at the larger fast-food franchisors. Here is an overview of the minority programs in place at KFC Corporation and Hardee's.

KFC Corporation.   Walt Simon, vice president, Business Development, at KFC says that the company has limited its recruitment efforts for new franchisees to ethnic minorities. Women franchisees are not being recruited because Mr. Simon says that "There is not a shortage of women in this business, either as sole owners or, often, as owners with their husbands."

The goal of KFC's program, according to Simon, is to help minorities build real wealth through the acquisition of land and restaurants. The main vehicle for the program is the guaranteed loan. KFC is guaranteeing loans for qualified minority buyers through the local banks and often with a preferred low interest rate.

The total financial outlay for a KFC outlet is $750,000 to $800,000. With the help of the guaranteed loan, the minority franchisee will normally pay off 50 percent of the investment in seven years. After seven years, if the business is successful, the franchisee will refinance the balance of the loan independently, and Simon reports that "about 92 percent of the participants have been successful." He adds that "many have gone on to become multiunit franchisees and board members of the various associations." Ultimately, KFC would like to have 12 to 15 percent minority franchisees.

Hardee's.   The company has a special program for minorities, currently offered only for African-Americans. Called the "Franchising Associates Program," it makes special provisions for training, financial assistance, and additional headquarters support. In the conventional program a net worth of $500,000—with $150,000 in liquid assets—is required of franchisees. The associate program has capital requirements of $55,000 in liquid assets.

After, the franchisee puts up the $55,000 initial investment, he or she attends a six-month mandatory management training program and then is entitled to lease and run a restaurant full-time for three years. At the end of the three-year lease period, the company will sell the equipment to the franchisee at net book value and will continue to lease the real estate.

Hardee's supplies the franchisee with considerable administrative support. During the three years, Hardee's handles all accounting, assists in personnel decisions, and pays bills out of the franchisee's account. Hardee's guarantees payment to vendors for the new franchise. It also helps out with management decisions. For example, a franchise director meets with the franchisee every 30 days to review costs and sales.

All these efforts are designed to help the new franchisee to arrive, after three years, to the point where he or she has accumulated $150,000 to $200,000 in cash and an established, successful restaurant. Thereafter, this franchisee can enter into a conventional franchise agreement with Hardee's by using bank financing. If, however, the new franchise is not completely viable after three years, Hardee's will give additional assistance, such as charging a lower monthly rent on the company-owned unit.

Government Programs

Although the franchise system itself is probably the most effective force for minority involvement, the federal government is also working to bring diverse groups into franchising. The U.S. Department of Commerce's Minority Business Development Agency (MBDA) has a nationwide network of centers set up to counsel minority individuals. According to Terrian Barnes-Bryant, the IFA's Minority and Women's Affairs spokesperson, the centers are all familiar with franchising. Barnes-Bryant says, "There is current information on franchising, and everyone at the centers is trained to help with business planning, networking, administration, as well as to generate opportunities for minority-owned firms. The personnel at the centers can help evaluate the franchise opportunity and assist in developing a business plan. Very importantly, the centers are well-connected in their communities and can help minorities get started." (See Appendix for addresses and telephone numbers.)

Tip

Be forewarned that the expertise varies from center to center. Also, some of the MBDA centers are understaffed and overburdened. If you contact a particularly busy center be prepared to call repeatedly, and don't give up until you speak to the right people.

State and Local Programs: A Starting Point

One of the very best places to look for managerial and financial help is the state and local programs. Most states have a division of business development specifically geared to minority and women's needs. Also, many states are showing a keen interest in franchise businesses as a way to promote commercial growth in the state.

Tip

We discovered that you have to ask for the definition of "minority" when contacting any of these state and local agencies. Sometimes "minority" is taken to mean ethnic minority and at other times the term includes women (in numbers not a minority) and yet at other times includes handicapped or disabled individuals. So first check to see that you are a part of the group they've designated "minority."

Maryland. The one state program that was routinely praised for its excellence is that of Maryland. Maryland pioneered a franchise financing assistance program designed specifically for minorities which, in Maryland, include ethnic minorities, women, and handicapped individuals. This program, the Maryland Equity Participation Investment Program (EPIP), approved by the state legislature in 1985, established an equity fund to assist minority purchases of franchises. EPIP is administered through the Maryland Small Business Development Financing Authority (MSBDFA).

The EPIP uses a variety of financial strategies such as long-term loans and guarantees, limited partnerships, and stock offerings. The program can provide up to 45 percent of the total business cost or a maximum of $100,000 for a term of seven years. The business owner is required to put up at least 10 percent of the total costs, and the state expects a reasonable return on its investment.

Besides the financial assistance, the program helps minorities to find and to evaluate franchise opportunities. More seasoned franchisees can receive assistance with their expansion efforts. For more information about these opportunities contact Randy Croxton (manager of Franchising Opportunities), Maryland Small Business Development Finance Authority, at (410) 333-4270.

Pennsylvania. Pennsylvania also has a program which aids minorities in their franchise choices. Through the Pennsylvania Minority Business Development Authority's Franchise Finance and Technical Assistance Program, the state offers long-term, low-interest loans of up to $750,000 to individuals investing $5000 to $50,000. Besides financial help, consultants provide free analysis of franchise opportunities for the applicant. For more information contact Nancy Chavez, Pennsylvania Department of Commerce, Pennsylvania Minority Business Development Authority, at (717) 783-1128.

New York. In New York, franchise loans are also available through its New York State Minority and Women Revolving Loan Fund of the Urban Development Corporation. As the title implies, both ethnic minorities and women may use this source. The amount of the loans range from $20,000 to $200,000, or twice the amount of the cash investment of the franchisee, whichever is less. Generally a minimum of 10 percent cash equity must be invested by the business owner. In addition, to qualify, the franchise system must be nationally known (with operations in at least three states and at least 15 franchise locations), and preference is given to franchises that are located in distressed areas. For more information contact Don Sutton, New York State Urban Development Corporation, at (212)930-0452.

Ohio.   At the Midwest Development Corporation (MIDCO)–Cincinnati/Dayton Franchise Development Project, your contact is Veronica Berry, P.O. Box 29405, Cincinnati, Ohio 45229, (513) 281-7814.

Florida.   At the Miami-Dade Franchise Technical Assistance Center of the Chamber of Commerce, your contact is Mr. Edwin Miller, Business Assistance Center, 6600 NW 27th Avenue, Miami, Florida 33147, (305) 693-3550. In addition, at the Jacksonville Franchise Development Program your contact is Patricia Ferm, Jacksonville Economic Development Company, 128 E. Forsyth St., Suite 500, Jacksonville, Florida 32202, (904) 630-1914.

If you are not based in Maryland, Pennsylvania, New York, Ohio, or Florida, contact the Office of Minority and Small Business Development in your state capitol. Virtually all the states, although in varying degrees of expertise, have some sort of program in place and will assist the minority small business owner.

Tip

Did you ever notice that you usually get more and better results—especially when dealing with a bureaucratic agency—if you do it *in person?* Whenever possible, try to set up a meeting with the key decision maker.

Support for Women

Women are becoming new business owners at twice the rate of men. If that statistic is surprising, here's another one: U.S. women wholly or partly own nearly one-third of all the franchise units in the United States and the number is rapidly increasing. In spite of these impressive numbers, many women still experience special problems in starting new businesses.

Women historically have found it much more difficult to get a loan. Even women with superior credit records will probably be asked to have a husband or a father cosign for a loan. Now, besides some of the programs already cited, there are agencies and organizations set up just to help women business owners overcome these obstacles and others. Most often these agencies exist mainly to advise and counsel women in business matters, rather than provide direct financial assistance. Even so, women can still benefit from them in a general way and use their expertise to plot the best course for obtaining financing.

The SBA has a program for women called the Office of Women's Business Ownership (OWBO). With 18 model centers throughout the United States, OWBO advises prospective business owners, conducts mentoring programs, and provides training and counseling. One of its most valuable functions is advice on capturing government contracts. For more information on the programs and location of the centers, call (202) 205-6673 or (202) 606-4000.

One of the better women's business organizations, although not specific to franchises, is the American Woman's Economic Development Corporation (AWED) at 71 Vanderbilt Ave., New York, New York 10169. AWED is a 15-year-old organization in part sponsored by a number of large corporations such as Citibank and AT&T and designed to deal with women's business progress and problems. There are three business counseling programs available. Two of the counseling programs are one-and-a-half hours long with an expert in the area where you need help. One is done in person in the NYC location, and the other is conducted by telephone for persons living outside the area. There is a minimal charge. The third program is a telephone hotline for an urgent question which can be answered by an expert in a maximum time of 10 minutes for a charge of $10. Comprehensive training programs are also offered which deal with topics such as starting and managing your own business. AWED is also known for its networking conferences and programs which nonmembers may attend. These functions are held in New York City,

Washington, D.C., Los Angeles, and a new location in Connecticut. Call (800) 222-2933 for information on all these services and programs.

Another influential women's organization is the National Association of Female Executives (NAFE). This is a membership organization which promises the following benefits: a voice in Washington through its ongoing lobbying efforts for women in business, networking opportunities, a bimonthly magazine, career development aids and seminars, and other savings, most notably access to financial and legal services at reasonable fees. Perhaps the biggest benefit for readers of this book, however, is the financial one. The NAFE Venture Capital Fund can provide you with up to $50,000 to start or expand your business. If your business plan is approved, NAFE will invest in your business. In addition, there is a credit-line program from which, if qualified, you can borrow up to $30,000. NAFE is at 127 W. 24th St., New York, New York 10011-1914.

A Powerful Program for Veterans

VetFran (as the Veterans Transition Franchise Initiative is known) was launched nationally in November of 1991 and is dedicated to making it easier for veterans to buy franchises. The founder, chairman, and driving force behind VetFran is Don Dwyer, the president of the Dwyer Group, which is an international conglomerate of franchised businesses based in Texas. Dwyer established VetFran as a cooperative effort of the International Franchise Association and Worldwide Franchise Consultants and participating franchisors. The franchisors each contribute $1000 per year which helps defray the cost of administering VetFran's national network of 1000 veterans groups, as well as lobbying efforts on behalf of veterans.

Current members of the Armed Forces will have up to 24 months following their discharge to begin participation in VetFran. All other veterans who can show proof of veteran's status (e.g., DD214) and have been discharged other than dishonorably can participate in VetFran. These qualified veterans have access to special incentives and support provided by VetFran's participating franchisors. For instance, about 130 franchise systems have agreed to discount their franchise fee by up to one-half or to finance up to 50 percent of the franchise fee at prevailing market rates. Some offer both options.

The prequalification required for VetFran participants is the same as for any other franchisee. As always, the franchisor evaluates the ability, credit history, and personal financial statement of the candidate. If the veteran does not have the capital requirements to purchase a franchise, however, the participating franchisor may provide in-house financing or may direct the prospective franchisee to an appropriate lender for a conventional or SBA-guaranteed loan.

Tip

Special concessions exist for certain categories of veterans. If the prospective franchisee is a Vietnam veteran or has a 30 percent or more compensable disability and has been turned down by a bank for both a conventional loan and an SBA-guaranteed loan, then the veteran may be eligible for a direct loan from SBA (ceiling of $150,000).

To get a better idea of how the VetFran program works, let's look at two participating franchisors. United Business Group operates two very young (almost start-up) franchise systems: the first, Military Rent-All, operates eight company stores and has four franchises, and the second, Marbles Music and Video, has seven franchise stores. For both systems, United Business Group will finance $7500 of the franchise fee for veterans. The second participating franchisor, Carvel, is a mature system and has numerous outlets nationwide. Tom Kornacki, director of Franchise Recruitment, says the company signed onto the program because "it brings us good candidates, with excellent qualifications." Carvel offers qualified veterans a 50 percent discount on the initial franchise fee (which ranges from $10,000 to $20,000, depending upon the program).

Besides signing up more franchisors to participate in VetFran, the organization is also working hard at enlisting government agency support. In addition, the organization encourages lending institutions to give veterans who are seeking to buy franchises special consideration. For more information on VetFran's program, contact Charlie Wood, administrator, at (817)753-4555.

Final Words

If you are a woman, a member of a minority, or a veteran you should fully explore all the special programs which have recently been developed to assist you toward your goal of owning a franchise business.

8

Up and Running

*My advice is to follow the system. That
really makes you successful, especially in
the first few years. Many of the franchises
not doing well don't follow the system.*
        LISA BRUMM
        *Formals Etc. (rental
        formalwear) franchisee*

A better title for this chapter might be "Up and Running—Almost."
Once you've chosen the franchise, signed the agreement, set up the
financing, and gone through training, you still have to:

- Choose the legal business form
- Negotiate real estate leases and rents
- Buy equipment and inventory
- Supervise structural changes and the "build-out"
- Recruit and select employees
- Plan local promotions and advertising

Each of these phases can have an impact on the success of your
start-up. This chapter will take you through the basic steps involved
and share a tip or two from some franchisees who have been there.

Choosing the Business Structure

You will have to choose among three basic business structures before you open your doors for business: the sole proprietorship, the partnership, and the corporation. Because each differs as to cost of setting up, tax consequences, and legal liability, I strongly advise you to consult with both an attorney and an accountant before making your decision. (See also Figure 8-1 at the end of this chapter for a comparative chart of various business structures.)

Sole Proprietorship

The sole proprietorship is simple and easy to organize. All you'll have to do is apply for a federal ID number and in many states obtain a state and/or municipal sales tax number. The expenses of starting a sole proprietorship are minimal because there is little legal documentation.

The sole proprietor owns all the stock of the business and keeps all the profits. However, the owner will also have to come up with all the capital to start and operate the business. Making decisions is easy; you don't have to consult with anyone else unless you want to. This is an advantage when quick responses to an opportunity is a necessity. The sole proprietor doesn't have to file a separate business income tax form. All the franchise income, expense, profit, and loss is transferred to the owner's personal tax return.

The biggest disadvantage of the sole proprietorship is the personal liability incurred from business operations. This structure offers no shelter from the claims of creditors. A successful law suit against a sole proprietor's business can result in a lien on the personal assets of the owner. Another disadvantage is that sole proprietorship makes no provision for the continuation of the business after the owner's death or retirement. There is no true continuity of management and ownership title.

Partnership

To qualify as a partnership, the franchise has to be owned by two or more persons who have a financial interest in the business. A partnership is easy to set up. In fact, it only requires two or more people agreeing to go into business together and doesn't even require a formal agreement—although a formal written agreement drawn up by an attorney is strongly advised.

A partnership, like a sole proprietorship, doesn't file a business tax return but is required to file an information return (Form 1065) signed by one of the partners. This form reports gross income, deductions, and the names of the owners with proportionate ownership. Each partner is liable for her or his commensurate share of the taxes resulting from the business. Unless a partnership agreement stipulates otherwise, profits and losses must be divided among partners according to their ownership ratio. Partners are personally responsible for the debts of the partnership, and the partnership will not shelter the participants from the personal liability of creditors' demands.

A partnership agreement should explicitly state the provisions for adjusting to the death or termination of a partner, otherwise, legally, the partnership is dissolved. The amount and method of payment for a partner's interest upon his termination or death should be specified in the agreement. Without this stipulation, a long and bitter confrontation is the usual outcome if the partnership is dissolved.

Tip

Choosing a partnership structure for your franchise business can be a hazardous decision. The most frightening aspect is the fact that you are not just responsible for your actions, as in a sole proprietorship, but can be held liable for the actions of any of your partners. And unlike a corporation, your personal assets can be confiscated for business judgments.

Corporation

A corporation is a group of individuals which is legally treated as a single person. It is a distinct entity and separate from that of its owners or stockholders. It is more costly and more time-consuming to set up than a sole proprietorship and a partnership. For example, a fee is payable at the time the charter or articles of incorporation are filed with the state agency. Additional costs include attorney's fees and other charges such as stock certificates and a corporate seal. You must get a federal ID number for use on federal tax returns and other documents. Also, you'll have to comply with state and local requirements for business licenses. The record keeping and reports for the corporation will be more complex than for a sole proprietorship or a partnership. Also, you will probably find that the required reports cause some loss of privacy and confidentiality.

The biggest plus for choosing a corporate structure is the limited liability. Personal liability is limited to the amount of money used to buy stock in the company, unlike the sole proprietorship and partnership, which put the participant's entire networth at risk for creditor satisfaction. Investors in a corporation avoid this total exposure. It's important to consult your attorney about fulfillment of your corporate responsibilities so that no one can "pierce the corporate veil" (the protection the corporate structure affords your personal assets is referred to as the "corporate veil"). Corporate responsibilities vary from state to state.

The corporation is unaffected by death or termination of a stockholder. However, the transfer or inheritance of stock can affect the ownership and control of the corporation. A corporation pays taxes much like an individual. It will file a tax return and will pay taxes on profits. The stockholders, in turn, will pay personal taxes on salaries and dividends.

There is a special entity called an "S corporation" which combines several of the advantages of both a partnership and a corporation. It is taxed like a partnership with gains and losses passed through to individual stockholders but without the personal liability that is associated with a partnership. However, the disadvantage is that loss deductions for tax purposes cannot exceed the amount a shareholder has invested in the business. For example, if you invest $100,000 in a corporation, that is the maximum amount you can deduct from your taxes as a loss. But with the partnership format, for example, you could invest the same amount ($100,000) but deduct $150,000 or more, if that is your share of the loss. In addition, a chapter S corporation is restricted to certain kinds of businesses and cannot have more than 35 stockholders.

Tip

It often pays to operate a business as an S corporation in the beginning years so that losses can be passed through to the shareholders for tax purposes. When the business becomes profitable, you can terminate the S status and elect the regular C corporate status.

Tip

Be very careful with timing if you want to elect S status or you will lose out. To be eligible, a new corporation must file for election in the 75-day period after the corporation has begun its first tax year. The beginning is defined as when the corporation issues stock to stockholders, acquires assets, or begins to do business—whichever occurs first.

How to Negotiate with the "Barracudas"

Once you have chosen a business structure, you can go on to decisions which relate to the operation of the franchise. If you're operating a retail business you probably have already settled on the location. One of the more difficult tasks still has to be tackled—negotiating a lease with a mall developer or landlord.

One franchisee said to me, "Mall developers are barracudas. You must learn to deal with them. It's very cutthroat." That certainly has not been the experience of every franchisee. You might be lucky enough to negotiate with very honest, cooperative, and accommodating landlords. But since being prepared is half the battle, here is some information and some suggestions to help you master the negotiations.

Tip

Signing a lease entails rights and obligations, so let your attorney review it before you sign anything. It's also a good idea to take along an expert from franchise management to help with lease negotiations. Lastly, consult your insurance agent to look into the responsibility for damage if you are leasing a space or a building.

All leases contain basic provisions such as rental amount, term of lease, commencement date, description of the premises, and renewal options. Beyond this, leases cover the specific needs and requirements of the landlord. It is in your best interest to read the lease carefully—along with your attorney—and negotiate those provisions that pose a problem for you.

Don't try to rush through the negotiations. They might not be easy or fun, but taking the time to make sure it's the best agreement for your business is worthwhile. I've talked to too many franchisees and heard too many stories about how they and others quickly signed a lease only to find themselves in a no-profit situation or even facing a business failure. Lisa Brumm, a Formals Etc. franchisee, has this advice for all potential lease signers: "If you want a location badly and you let it show, you won't be able to negotiate. You must be able to walk away from the table. It may be the perfect mall or office building, but most likely there are other good ones out there."

Tip

Wee-bag-it owner Marcy Pinnell, with the expert help of the franchisor, was able to negotiate an "18-month kick-out clause" with the landlord. The clause stipulates that if her business is not profitable within 18 months she can give up the five-year lease and pay three or four months' rent in a lump sum as settlement to the landlord. Try this—with the franchisor's assistance.

Aside from questioning the costs and benefits of the existing lease clauses, pay attention to the following:

1. Coordinate the term of the real estate lease with the term of the franchise agreement. For example, if your franchise agreement is for five years, try to sign the lease for five years.

2. Ask the landlord to write in lease renewal options.

3. Note the date that rent commences. If possible, try not to pay any rent before the premises are ready for occupancy. For example, you do not want to pay the rent while the space is getting painted or the equipment and fixtures are getting installed.

4. Ask for a few months of free rent in return for signing a long-term lease.

5. Be sure there is a clause allowing you the right to assign or sublet the premises in case you decide to sell the franchise.

6. Negotiate hard to pay a fixed rent rather than a percentage rent. Percentage rents usually work like this: The franchisee pays a minimum rent until his or her business hits a target gross sales figure, at which point a higher rent based on a percentage of gross sales kicks in.

Tip

If you absolutely can't escape a percentage rent clause (shopping center management can be adamant about this), put your efforts into negotiating the very highest gross sales escalation point you can. For example, push for the percentage rent to tick in at $300,000 rather than $200,000.

7. Ask for exclusivity clauses that prevent competing businesses from operating in the same location.

8. Negotiate with the landlord to participate in the cost of signage and structural work.

In some cases you may find that arranging a lease entails dealing with the franchisor, not the mall developer or landlord. Some franchisees pay rent to the franchisors, who hold the leases. Often the rent is paid monthly, calculated on the basis of gross sales. This, too, is a percentage rent so be careful. In another scenario, the franchisor builds the premises for the franchisee and then leases it back to the franchisee. Alternatively, the franchisor may build and then sell the premises to a sale-and-leaseback company who will then become the franchisee's landlord.

Trap

If the landlord and the franchisor are one and the same, don't assume she or he has your best interests at heart. Negotiate these leases as carefully as you would with any landlord.

Installing the Inner Workings

After you've settled rents and leases to your satisfaction, you'll have some decisions to make about store design, equipment, and inventory. The franchisors often set certain specifications and limits. To meet these guidelines and to accommodate your business needs, you might need to make some structural changes in the leased space before opening.

Tip

Be sure the space is suitable for your business. One franchisee told how a food product had to be made fresh daily, but the space did not lend itself to efficient production. If it takes 25 percent more time, for example, to perform a task or to produce a product because the space is not appropriate, your bottom line will certainly suffer.

The time it takes to select and install the most suitable equipment and furniture will correspond indirectly with the age and sophistication of the system you're buying into. The older, larger franchise systems usually have the outfitting of the premises practically down to a science. Everything should be mapped out for you in terms of the best equipment, where to place it, and how to install it. In contrast, one of the newer systems or a start-up franchise will not have such tried and true suggestions. Ken Wisotzky remembers that when he opened his My Favorite Muffin franchise, the franchisor didn't help with the placement and installation of the baking equipment. He was pretty much on his own and had to work out logistical problems by trial and error.

Tip

"Don't invest in showy offices, taking clients to lunch, and Christmas gifts," says Larry Gambino, Priority Management franchisee, "it's more important to give good customer service."

Tip

Jim Gendreau, a Cost Cutters multiple-unit franchisee, says, "Be conservative in your office. For example, my corporate office is furnished with cheap furniture. Why? I only invest in things that make money. Furniture doesn't make money."

Calculating inventory requirements can also be a trial-and-error process. Ken Wisotzky had two sets of inventory problems with his side-by-side franchises in a retail shopping mall. In the Gloria Jean's coffee store, he found that he bought too much inventory because he opened the store during its slowest month. Based on that experience, he advises others to study the sales figures or to talk to other franchisees to find out the buying patterns and to adjust your opening inventory accordingly.

Meanwhile, in Wisotzky's My Favorite Muffin franchise, the inventory problem was even more complex. With the muffins—or any food product made fresh daily—you have to guess at the quantity, and in this case, the flavors. In the beginning, Wisotzky says, "There was a lot of waste because we weren't too sure what and how much our clientele would buy. But now (after over four years) there's almost no waste."

In other instances inventory decisions can involve staffing problems as well. For example, Florence and George Hayden had to decide not only how much fresh food to prepare but how much time they would need to prepare it. After a few days of operation, they realized they had to have the staff in their Wendy's restaurant in at 7 a.m. for a 10:30 to 11 a.m. opening. Chili, for example, takes four hours to cook (they figured out later that it could be cooked the night before), and slicing onions, lettuce, and other vegetables for the salad bar took a few hours, even with four to six people working.

Tip

Time the opening of your business carefully. Many franchisees advised against opening the business at the busiest time of year. Most felt they needed an easing in period first. First impressions can be lasting impressions. You may not have a second chance with customers if they encounter poor or inefficient service or an untrained staff.

Managing the "Build-Out"

When talking about construction and structural changes, called the "build-out," we often heard words like *horrible* and *nightmarish*. Those reactions were conjured by snafus such as:

- The franchisor's estimated set-up costs are based on the costs of goods, services, and labor in a cheaper region. Be aware of wide variations in pricing for different parts of the country.

- Unanticipated local and government regulations can add charges or changes for the franchisee.

- Unethical constructions crews who do a poor job can inflate the costs.

Most franchise systems are adjusting their estimates to reflect that construction costs are higher in some areas, especially in the New York City metropolitan area and in certain areas of California. Union labor costs were mentioned often as being one of the reasons for disparate costs in the country. Even so, if you are in a part of the country where costs are traditionally higher, take the franchisor's high-end estimate and add 10 percent to arrive at your probable build-out costs.

Trap

Jeff Grayson, a multiunit Pizzeria Uno franchisee, found his franchisor's estimated costs were too low because it did "not calculate sales tax and installation charges for equipment in the initial costs." In Grayson's case, this added an additional 15 percent to the estimated costs and, at times, could add as much as 20 percent.

Another thing to do before beginning work on the build-out is to look into municipal codes. Leslie Goldberg and her partner Mark Weintraub opened their Expressions Custom Furniture franchise in a new strip center in a completely empty building. Consequently, they had to construct walls, put in electrical wiring, and take care of other basics. Conforming to the numerous building codes and regulations covering this light construction added extra time and extra costs to the construction.

Government regulations can also be a source of added expense. During the construction of the Hayden's second Wendy's restaurant, an inspector from a federal government agency visited the construction site and informed them that there was not proper access for handicapped persons. To comply with the regulation stipulating that handicapped persons should not have to cross any traffic to gain entrance to a business, the Haydens had to stop construction and revise their plans.

Hiring the wrong people to work on your build-out can be the biggest nightmare of all. One franchisee came from a state on the West coast where the construction people are bonded and don't get paid until the work is satisfactorily finished. This was not the case when the husband and wife franchisees did extensive construction on a store in the Northeast. They now find themselves enmeshed in a tough lawsuit because although they paid the general contractor, he didn't pay the subcontractors, who are now demanding payment from the franchisee.

You can avoid these problems by getting referrals on all the general construction people before you hire them. Then, don't do anything structurally until you talk to the architect, the plumber, the electrician, and the carpenter, to be sure all know what they are doing. Go over the plans with each worker to be certain the plans make sense. Then firm up all the costs and get them in writing. You may have to pay some up-front money for materials, but don't pay the entire agreed-upon sum until everything is done to your satisfaction.

Tip

George Lawson, a franchise owner with Robin Sparks of Red Hot & Blue, a barbeque restaurant, says, "Try to find a failed restaurant site. You can save a lot of money by using old restaurant premises. For example, the air-conditioning, all the services from the street, much of the kitchen equipment, toilets, sewage, and so on are there. Restaurant owners can save 30 to 40 percent by going into a shell. That frees up more cash for the front of the house instead of sinking it into buried sewer pipes and the like." Here's another way to save money: If the kitchen equipment has not been installed and is not proscribed or leased by the franchisor, try to buy it at an auction. You may end up paying as little as 25 percent of the standard price for slightly used equipment.

Employees: The Heart of the Business

Ideally, you're going to hire people who are not only good workers—capable, energetic, conscientious—but also people you like. If you spend 40 to 60 hours a week together, it really helps if you like each other.

Every business has a slightly different twist on selecting, hiring, and retaining employees, but, in general, we found franchisees were looking for help with high turnover rates, motivating employees, training them, and finding ones with specialized skills.

Franchisees were particularly eager to find out how to bring out the best in their low-wage employees. For instance, Tom Orban, an I Can't Believe It's Yogurt (ICBY) franchisee, says, "It's difficult to get the right employee. Of course it's important to motivate employees. But how do you motivate employees who are being paid a minimum wage?" Meanwhile, another franchisee noted that, "If you haven't been accustomed to working with minimum wage people you will find it difficult to deal with. They have different needs and desires than you and me and are mostly living from month to month." She goes on to say that she did find better skill levels with older people and women (more meticulous with details). And a Subway franchisee found that, "Employees working for low wages don't always care about giving the best service."

Tip

Here's a great idea to use when you start out and need sales but have little money for employees. Fred Banty and five other Connecticut Padgett Business Services franchisees joined together to hire one salesperson to prospect for sales. The six share the cost of one salesperson and, so far, they are pleased with the results.

Motivation, in part, seems to stem from the economic situation of your region of the country. In areas where jobs are highly valued or there is a high unemployment rate, there seems to be no problem filling the ranks with motivated employees. For example, George Hayden finds there is no problem staffing his two Wendy's restaurants in northeast Pennsylvania. So far the work force has been extremely stable probably because jobs—even minimum wage ones—are not plentiful in the area. Another franchisee in the same region, Danny Kostick with eleven Pizza Hut restaurants, agrees that finding good employees in the region is not a problem even though he requires about 300 to 350 part-time workers to staff the different locations.

Tip

Many franchisees utilize part-time workers in their businesses not only because it fits the ebbs and flows of the business but also because part-time employees are cheaper, since they normally don't get benefits.

Some franchisees need employees with specialized skills, and that isn't always easy. Kitty Alaily, a multiunit franchisee of Cost Cutters and City Lights hair salons has "an average of 6 to 8 employees per store but could often use 13 to 14." She explains that central Wisconsin has a tight labor supply and that "the labor pool of qualified hairdressers is fought over by all the hair salons."

Glenn Schenenga also has a difficult time finding the right employees. To operate his Futurekids franchise, he needs very special employees, ones that are "certified teachers who have P/C skills and also must be able to market the services as well as teach. They need a certain style, and old-fashioned teachers don't seem to work. It's difficult to find teachers who will make it fun for the kids to learn computer skills."

Once a franchisee has found the right employee, there's the age-old problem of retaining good employees and keeping turnover to a minimum. Sometimes, employees join the franchisor for a short-term goal. For instance, many Jani-King (commercial cleaning) employees do that work as a sideline to their day jobs. Carla Cunningham, a Jani-King franchisee, says "Often when employees achieve their money goal they quit." This franchise has had its best luck with recent high school graduates, since they pay a little above minimum wage. And, the company is attacking the high turnover problem by constantly scouting for new employees for their database so they're prepared for additional business.

Then there are some businesses in which the franchisee must spend what seems to be an inordinate time dealing with employees' issues. Jeanette Fuller, a Tutor Time franchisee, says, "Dealing with employees is a major part of running a day-care center for children 6 weeks to 5 years old." Fuller considers staffing her biggest challenge. Employees find it difficult to work eight hours a day with toddlers, and so Fuller primarily hires part-timers who can keep their enthusiasm level high for the shorter time. Employees who call in "sick" often is another problem, since she has to try and replace the person on short notice.

Tip

College campuses are a great source for good part-time employees. Joan Maruyama, A Choice Nanny franchisee in the Washington, D.C., area, suggests calling local universities for business students. She finds they're especially good at doing marketing projects.

Planning Local Promotions and Advertising

When you open a new business you want everyone to know about it. Even better, you'd like a lot of people to try out your product or service. To that end, depending upon your choice of franchise, you may have to do a lot or a little promotion. If your franchise is part of a start-up system or only has a few franchises, you'll have to create an identity through a local promotional campaign that tells potential customers about the product or service you're offering. However, in the case of one of the nationally known franchises, you'll do less on a local level because the instant name recognition will bring customers to you. In both the cases, though, franchisees will do some local advertising and promotions to launch new businesses.

Finding the best ways to advertise and promote products and services is mainly a process of trial and error. No doubt, in the beginning, mistakes are made. You might find, like Fred Banty of Padgett

Business Services, that local advertisements don't work as well as cold calls, telemarketing, and referrals do for finding customers. Leslie Goldberg, an Expressions Custom Furniture franchisee in a New York City suburban community finds that advertising can bring business but reports that, "We spent too much money on advertising and got very little impact for it at first." Over the past two years, she has refined her advertising placements by asking every person who walks into the furniture store where they heard or read about the store. In this way, she can tell which advertisements had the best draw.

Timing promotions for major impact and the best results is another challenge. Prior to opening their Wendy's franchise, Florence and George Hayden promoted the store opening heavily. They advertised extensively in local newspapers and announced free prizes at the opening. Then, they had some public relations nights. One was a "parents night" where all the parents of the workers were invited and the employees served and practiced on the parents. A "VIP Night" was next where they invited the contractors, community leaders, clergy, family, and friends.

In the end, all this advertising and promotion worked too well! George Hayden says, "For over four weeks the business was so strong that the staff couldn't keep up. The kids were so tired that they called in sick after four days." (The Haydens did win a sales prize from Wendy's for top opening week sales.) This experience leads them to advise other franchisees to open up a store without much fanfare and then, a week or so later, have a grand opening after most of the bugs are out.

Tip

To make all openings go smoother, hire a key person—someone with a good deal of industry experience—to head up your staff.

Final Words

Starting up a business—even one in which procedures and specifications are almost down to a science—can feel like being on a roller coaster. The ups and downs are completely normal, and as long as you continue to make major decisions methodically and carefully, you will avoid serious problems.

Establishment of Business Form and Operation	
Proprietorship	Least complicated to create and operate. Not considered a separate legal entity from owner/operator.
General partnership	Separate legal entity created. Desirable to have formal written agreement regarding all partners. Relatively simple to establish.
Limited partnership	More complicated than general partnership. Requires written agreement between partners. Creates at least two classes of partners. General partners bear sole responsibility for management.
Regular corporation	Separate legal entity that requires formality in creation and operation. May have several classes of shareholders.
S corporation	Same as regular corporation except restrictions exist regarding types of qualifying shareholders and classes of stock.
Limited liability companies	Not available in all states. Requires formal written agreement. May be treated as a partnership depending upon certain characteristics.
Liability for Debts of Business Activity	
Proprietorship	Unlimited personal liability exists.
General partnership	General partners have unlimited liability.
Limited partnership	Same as general partnership except limited partners generally liable only to the extent of their investment.
Corporation	Stockholders generally liable only to extent of capital investment; however, stockholders may be required to personally guarantee corporate borrowings. In addition, under certain circumstances, "responsible party" stockholders may be liable for unremitted or underwithheld payroll taxes.
Limited liability companies	Generally same treatment as limited partnership where all "members" have limited liability.

Figure 8-1. Characteristics of Various Business Structures.

Federal Income Taxation of Business Profits	
Proprietorship	Taxed to individual owner at graduated rates of 15%, 28%, 31%, and 36%. Note: In some cases, new 10% surcharge may apply. Also subject to self employment taxes.
Partnerships	Taxed to partners at individual or corporate rates depending on tax status of partner.
Regular corporation	Corporate entity pays tax at graduated rates of 15% on first $50,000 of taxable income, 28% on next $25,000 of taxable income, and 34% over $75,000 of taxable income. A 5% surcharge is imposed on taxable incomes over $100,000 to eliminate the benefit of the lower brackets. A higher rate is now imposed on very large corporations.
S corporation	Generally taxed to individual owners at their respective tax rates. However, in certain cases a corporate level tax may exist.
Limited liability companies	Generally taxed as a partnership.

Potential for Double Taxation Upon Withdrawal of Business Profits (for Federal Tax Purposes)	
Proprietorship	None
Partnerships	None
Regular corporation	Yes, to extent payments exceed reasonable compensation limits to employee/stockholders.
S corporation	Generally, none.
Limited liability companies	Generally, none.

Deduction of Business Losses by Owners	
Proprietorship	Generally, yes. Must be cognizant of "hobby loss" rules.

(Continued)

Figure 8-1. *(Continued)*

Partnerships	Yes. Limited partners losses usually cannot exceed capital investment. "At risk" rules must be considered.
Regular corporation	No. Losses remain with corporate entity to offset corporate earnings. Loss carryback and carryover provisions exist.
S corporation	Generally, yes, provided the shareholders have sufficient basis for absorbing losses.
Limited liability companies	Generally, yes. Members may deduct losses in accordance with "at risk" provisions.
Social Security and Medicare Tax Imposed on Business Profits	
Proprietorship	Combined rate of 15.3% applied to "self employment" earnings up to a certain amount. Medicare portion of 2.9% applies without limit. Individual receives a deduction for a portion of this amount in arriving at adjusted gross income.
Partnerships	Self employment taxes imposed on individual partners on "self employment earnings" that flow through the partnership. Same limits as proprietorship.
Corporations	Combined rate of 15.3% is shared equally by employee/stockholders and corporation.
Limited liability companies	Generally, same treatment as partnerships.
Unemployment Taxes Imposed on Business Profits	
Proprietorship	None.
Partnerships	None.
Corporations	Yes. Generally federal and state unemployment taxes apply to compensation paid to employee/stockholders.
Limited liability companies	Generally, none.

Figure 8-1. (*Continued*)

Retirement Plans	
Proprietorship	Keogh plan and Simplified Employee Pension (SEP) Plan available. Generally same features as corporate plans available to unincorporated entities.
Partnerships	Same as for sole proprietorships.
Regular corporation	Generally no distinction from plans available to unincorporated entities. Participant borrowings permitted.
S corporation	Same rules apply as for regular corporations. However, participant borrowings not permitted to 2% or greater shareholder.
Limited liability companies	Generally, same as partnerships.
Tax Treatment of Fringe Benefits	
Proprietorship	25% of medical insurance premium deducted in arriving at adjusted gross income. Other items must be evaluated independently based on existing tax laws.
Partnerships	Various treatment applies to different fringe benefits that may be paid by the partnership on behalf of a partner. A tax advisor should be consulted.
Regular corporation	Generally deductible by corporation and not taxable to employee.
S corporation	Special rules apply to fringe benefits paid on behalf of a 2% or greater shareholder. A tax advisor should be consulted.
Limited liability companies	Generally, same as partnerships.
SOURCE: Richard A. Clapsaddle, CPA.	

Figure 8-1. (*Continued*)

9

Franchise Trends and Opportunities

I find that it takes less time to run eleven restaurants—which I manage—rather than one which I used to work in and manage.   DANNY KOSTICK
                    Pizza Hut franchisee

The 1990s will see enormous growth and change in franchising as more and more Americans decide to try their hand at running their own business. The increasing number of franchisees who are subfranchisors, area developers, and especially multiunit owners is one trend that's likely to continue. It's entirely possible that a good percentage of the franchise owners by the year 2000 will be owning and operating a sizeable corporate entity, rather than the Mom-and-Pop businesses commonly associated with franchising. Another accelerating trend is the number of independent businesses which *convert* to a franchise. No doubt you have heard of Century 21, the real estate company. Century 21, with 7000 franchised outlets worldwide, expands largely by converting existing businesses to their franchise system. This is a very visible example of conversion franchising, and you may be surprised to hear about all the new franchises that are using this technique to grow their businesses.

Understanding the Terms

Before taking a closer look at the trends, you need to understand the terminology. The following is a brief guide to the most common concepts.

Subfranchisor

A franchisee who is granted the right to exercise powers normally reserved for the franchisor—in a specific territory—is a *subfranchisor.* A separate initial fee is usually charged to the subfranchisor for the right to subfranchise an area or territory. Subfranchisors have the right to offer and sell franchises and to collect fees and royalties. They then have to provide training services and support to franchisees within the boundaries of their designated territories. The subfranchisor signs a subfranchise agreement with the franchisor and will also enter into a franchise agreement with franchisees (when a franchise is sold) in the specified territory.

The fees which are collected by the subfranchisor may be split between the subfranchisor and the franchise system, or, in some cases, the subfranchisor will retain a majority of the fees. The subfranchise agreement spells out the amount of the franchise fee and royalty each will receive. This can be an extremely lucrative arrangement for the subfranchisor, but keep in mind that subfranchisors first have to spend heavily to sign up subfranchisees in their territories.

Depending on the agreement, the subfranchisor may operate one unit, several units, or no units at all in the territory. Often the development of the territory is subject to a quota or schedule. The goal objectives may be measures such as franchise agreements executed, units open and operating, or units "under construction." For example, the agreement may state that within two years after the contract is signed, the subfranchisor must have a minimum of five units open and operating or lose the exclusive territory. Subfranchisors can satisfy all or part of their goals by opening units themselves.

Not every franchise system offers subfranchisor agreements. It doesn't suit the organization of every franchise business. Then, too, many systems simply don't like the loss of power that goes with subfranchising. Naturally, subfranchisors wield more power over the franchisor than do individual franchisees because subfranchisors control a larger number of units and are responsible for a greater amount of the system's revenue.

From a subfranchisor's standpoint, the deal isn't always perfect. Subfranchisors often run a substantial financial risk, since the investment needed to purchase a territory can be large. Also, since subfranchisors sell franchises, they are exposed to future litigation from disgruntled franchisees. Those risks and headaches, however, are offset by the greater rewards available to subfranchisors. They will share in the initial fees for new franchisees and the royalty payments, which continue for the life of a franchise agreement—maybe 10, 20 years or more.

Tip

A useful by-product of subfranchising is a solution to one of the franchisee's biggest challenges—finding and keeping good employees. Stuart and Sharon Ruben signed a subfranchising agreement for the Money Mailer franchise system, a business of direct mail advertising, not only because they believed they would be able to go out and sell the franchise concept in their territory but also because they decided the franchisees they signed up would be better motivated to succeed (because their money is in it) than a number of hired sales people in offices they would be obliged to open in the area. So far the Rubens operate one area office themselves and have twelve subfranchisees which they service and train.

Area Developers

A franchisee who has the right to establish and operate more than one unit within a defined territory is an *area developer*. Unlike a subfranchisor, an area developer does not sell or service franchises in an exclusive area. The area developer will usually pay a fee for the territorial rights and will have a performance obligation or schedule for development.

The obligation to open a certain number of units in the designated territory, within a certain period, poses some challenges for area developers. First of all, they must have the financial and managerial capability to develop multiple units. Sometimes, an area agreement will allow the area developer to bring in investors through limited partnerships for the ownership and financing of individual units. However, the area developer remains as the sole general partner.

Aside from financing, questions regarding performance requirements can be the basis of some potential problems. One is the question of units in a territory which are opened and subsequently closed. Are these units counted toward completion of the development schedule? And what happens to the area developer who fulfills performance obligations ahead of schedule? Under most agreements, that developer will be penalized by losing exclusive rights to the territory earlier than expected. One way to avert this problem is to request a right of first refusal for any additional development proposed for your territory. In any case, these points need to be negotiated before the agreement is signed.

Area developers, like subfranchisors, also wield a good deal of power over the franchisor compared to individual unit owners. The franchisor will usually try to keep the upper hand by stipulating in the agreement that if performance requirements are not reached by the area developer, the franchise corporation can repurchase the franchise.

Area Representative

This arrangement developed, in part, so that franchisors could have the benefit of subfranchising without giving up the control that they give up in a subfranchisor relationship. The *area representative* usually pays the franchisor a fee for the right to solicit prospective franchisees and to provide certain services to existing franchisees in a defined territory. Once an area "rep" finds a new franchisee, the area rep does not enter into contracts with the franchisee, unlike the subfranchisor. Rather, all franchise agreements are entered into directly between the franchisor and the franchisee. Likewise, the initial fees and royalties are paid directly to the franchisor.

What's in it for the area representative? The franchisor pays the area rep a portion of the initial franchise fees as compensation for finding franchisees (essentially a sales commission) and a portion of the royalties received for servicing franchisees. In some cases, franchisors will pay area reps a portion of the fee received from new franchisees in the reps' territory even though an area rep had nothing to do with screening and recommending that particular franchisee. Of course, all this and other contingencies—such as compensation for furnishing many of the preopening and ongoing services to the franchisee—should be covered in the area representation agreement.

Most often the area representative is also a franchisee in the defined territory, owning one or multiple units. The area rep may own 100 percent of one unit or may have a smaller ownership in several units.

Linda Moore, previously a senior corporate executive, likes the area representative arrangement she has with Ledger Plus, a franchise which offers accounting, tax planning, and tax preparation to small businesses. In particular she likes that she "is compensated almost immediately for her efforts, with a cashflow from the beginning," that comes from the portion of the initial fee and royalties she receives for signing up franchisees. In addition, she says, "I hope to have a steady annuity stream from the royalties I'll be paid. Also, this will be an equity-type business which will be saleable at some time."

Tip

You may find slightly different names used for the area representative arrangement. For example, Linda Moore signed on as a "regional representative" for Ledger Plus, but, despite the slightly different name, it fits our definition of area representative. The important thing is for you to find out exactly your relationship to the franchisor and your responsibilities and compensation.

When asked about all the time involved in recruiting franchisees, servicing them, and operating her own franchise, Linda said, "It's not a problem. In the beginning most of the work was in recruiting new franchisees for my territory, so there's no support function to worry about. Now I'm getting into the support function also, but eventually the recruiting will stop and all my efforts [besides running her own franchise] will go to supporting franchisees in my territory."

Linda, coming out of a corporate business background herself, thinks that area representation is a good opportunity for excorporate workers to consider. "It provides someone coming from a business development background a way to use his or her skills," she says.

Linda adds that she wouldn't want to just sell franchises. It's the whole equation—sales, support, and operation of her own franchise—that makes it a rewarding challenge.

Tip

Many single-unit franchise owners complain of not earning enough money. If you have the managerial abilities and the financial resources, owning multiple locations is a way to make a considerable amount of money.

Multiple-unit Owner

In the United States about 20 percent of franchisees are *multiple-unit owners*. In our own informal survey of franchisees, we found that 34 percent are multiple-unit owners. Owning and operating more than one unit is clearly a trend and one that most franchise systems are encouraging.

Although the subfranchisor, the area developer, and the area representative may own multiple units, a multiple-unit owner doesn't have to fall into one of these three categories. A multiple franchise unit owner is simply someone who owns and operates more than one location. The multiple-unit owner hires a manager for each of the individual locations and oversees the general management of all the various locations.

Trap

Be very careful that you know exactly what you're doing in the first unit of your franchise business before seriously considering multiple-unit ownership. For example, you should have an efficient accounting system up and running, as well as systems for controlling costs and analyzing sales before you open your second and third locations. As one multiple-unit franchisee found out, "It's difficult to correct bad habits."

It isn't necessary to buy an area or region to open multiple units. If you don't, however, you run the risk that by the time you're thinking about opening a second franchise unit, the area you're interested in may be taken or might be saturated. Sometimes you can avoid these problems by getting a written commitment from the franchisor giving you the right of first refusal to a nearby location that it plans to develop. It's generally easier to get such a commitment from the newer franchise systems.

Tip

Jeff Grayson, a Pizzeria Uno area developer, advises, "Don't buy territories. Open up each restaurant [or unit of whatever the business] and try to be successful. Focus on each one. Don't be overly concerned about someone else coming in and opening up the same franchise in your area."

Master Franchisee

To complete the terminology, a *master franchisee* is actually the same as a subfranchisor, except on a bigger scale. The term, used in international franchising (an increasingly popular area of franchising), describes a subfranchisor whose territory is a foreign country or a portion of it. If you are interested in exploring this opportunity, refer to Chapter 10 for details.

Tip

Here's a variation on the multiple-unit ownership you might like to consider: Rather than buying a number of units from the same franchisor, think about buying a variety of franchise businesses in an area or region. For example, you may own and operate five fast-food restaurants, two retail photo shops, and three car repair services, all in the same area. In that way, you're diversifying businesses—probably decreasing your financial risk—and building a mini business empire at the same time.

Converting an Independent Business to a Franchise Unit

Converting an existing independent business to a franchised unit of a franchise system is clearly an accelerating trend. Right now about

40 percent of all franchisors offer conversion franchises. This section will look at the opportunities behind the growing popularity of conversion franchises.

In general terms, there are trade-offs for both the franchisee and franchisor. For the independent-owner-turned-franchisee there's the advantage of the franchisor's broader name recognition, the increased marketing and advertising clout, and the lower product and supply costs. Those benefits might outweigh the control and independence that the conversion franchisee forfeits. By taking on a conversion franchisee, the franchisor gains an experienced business owner with a track record and loses a competitor. Many franchisors believe, though, that they are taking a risk because it is a very difficult mental adjustment to go from independent to franchisee, and consequently some conversion franchisees might never succeed in making the switch.

Another reason business owners might join a franchise is that the franchisor's product or service is superior to their own. Lisa Brumm was running a bridal dress sales business in Litchfield, Illinois, when she got an invitation to participate in a gown rental convention in Chicago. There she met the owners of Formals Etc., a completely new franchise. She was intrigued by their business idea—renting bridal gowns and other formal wear—so she spent the next six months studying and researching Formals Etc. Lisa came up with three reasons for converting her independent business to a Formals Etc. franchise. First, she wasn't making money at her business selling gowns. Second, there was a market need for rentals. And third, her own personal experiences confirmed her gut feeling about the new business. She remembered her husband renting a tux for the numerous weddings where she was a bridesmaid while she bought a costly dress that she would never wear again. Lisa is happy she decided to become a franchisee, and she opened her second shop in December of 1992. She learned quickly that following the franchise system is a necessity even though she finds "it's still hard having someone else to answer to."

Sharon Taylor, another recent conversion franchisee, made the switch for the sake of a new challenge. After seventeen years of running an independent bath and soap shop in New Mexico, Sharon decided it was time for a change. At first, she thought about going into a different industry. Then after looking at a variety of franchises for over a year, she realized she wanted to stay in the body care business, which she already knew. Luckily she found a franchise that differed only slightly from her previous business but still offered a change. The franchise, Potions and Lotions, sold private label body care products and custom-made fragrances, did not use animals to test its products, and was committed to recycled packaging. All this appealed to Sharon. Although she is enjoying her new shop, Sharon admits that "it took a lot of mental adjustment to commit herself to pay someone for the idea, pay a royalty and then do all the required paperwork. The process of finally making the decision to buy the franchise was slow and painful."

Final Words

Franchising, as a business concept, is evolving in the 1990s to accommodate the needs, objectives, and talents of the new franchisee. Many new franchisees use a franchise to build a good-sized business in which they can utilize all their managerial skills.

10
Expanding to International Markets

There are remarkable opportunities in
Hungary and the other Eastern European
countries for service franchise businesses,
because just about every service is needed.
GEORGE HEMINGWAY
international franchisee

International franchising is an increasingly popular area of franchising. According to Bob Jones at the International Franchise Association (IFA), about 20 percent of the U.S. franchise systems operate in markets outside the country, and, when polled, 97 percent of those say they will increase the number of foreign markets entered; 50 percent of the remaining franchise systems say they are making plans to enter international markets in the near future.

The franchise most known for its international expansion is probably McDonald's. McDonald's is seen as a goodwill ambassador and a purveyor of U.S. culture in such diverse cities as Moscow and Bejing and has helped pave the way for other franchise systems to follow. Already, companies such as AlphaGraphics, Futurekids, Fuddruckers, Haagen-Dazs, and many others are established in countries out-

157

side the United States and continue to actively seek international franchisees.

As you might expect, U.S. franchises are most heavily represented in Canada, Mexico, and the United Kingdom, primarily because of proximity and/or language. In the last few years, however, the franchise trend has become truly global. Franchising is booming in Asian markets such as Japan, Taiwan, and Hong Kong, and Latin American countries like Brazil, Chile, and Columbia. Franchising businesses are also well-entrenched in Western European countries, and serious inroads are being made in the former Soviet-bloc countries like Hungary, Poland, and the Czech and Slovak Republics. (Refer to Figure 10-1 to get an idea of the franchising numbers in Europe.)

Unlike the United States, there is little franchise regulation in most of these countries. Only Alberta (Canada), Mexico, and France have franchise laws, and Australia has a self-regulatory structure. As of now there seems to be little interest on the part of government or potential franchisees to regulate franchises outside the United States. This means you will have to be doubly careful about doing all the preliminary work and analysis before choosing to operate a franchise system in a country where no franchise regulation exists.

Country	Number of franchisors	Number of franchisees
Austria	80	2,500
Belgium	90	3,200
Denmark	42	500
France	600	30,000
Germany	265	9,950
Republic of Ireland	20	—
Italy	318	16,100
Netherlands	309	11,005
Norway	125	3,500
Portugal	55	800
Spain	117	14,500
Sweden	200	9,000
United Kingdom	373	18,100
SOURCE: The European Franchise Federation.		

Figure 10-1. Franchising in Europe.

Tip

Most of the world franchise market is where the United States was 10 or 15 years ago. Global opportunities are plentiful.

Candidates for International Franchising

This book will be read in many countries outside the United States. If you are an individual living in a country other than the United States you will find information in this chapter which will help you to understand the mechanics and the special considerations of buying a U.S. franchise to operate in your country. You may also consider buying native franchise systems, which are fairly well represented in countries such as Canada and those of Western Europe.

Tip

For individuals seeking permanent resident status (PRS) in the United States, there is now a way to combine an interest in franchising with PRS. The 1990 U.S. Immigration Act created a new category of immigrant visas. Under the act's provisions, a foreign citizen who buys a franchise in the United States may receive the "green card" which provides PRS.

It requires an investment of $500,000 to $3 million, depending on location and regional unemployment conditions. For those unable to invest $500,000, one could qualify for the E-2 visa or "treaty investor." This requires a "substantial" investment but not necessarily $500,000. In addition, the capital which is invested must directly benefit the U.S. economy and employ at least 10 U.S. citizens.

If you are interested in these business visas and have a desire to purchase a U.S. franchise, you should contact the U.S. embassy in your country.

A former corporate employee in the United States with an international business expertise might also want to explore international franchising. Besides the professional experience, the candidate should have a great deal of familiarity with the targeted foreign market and be well-acquainted with a host of business contacts in the country.

When Bob Jones at the IFA was asked whether a U.S. resident could feasibly consider becoming a master franchisee for a foreign country, he answered, "Yes, but it is rare. The franchisor wants to have a local partner who has a strong connection with the culture." This means the franchisee would have to live most of the time in the targeted country. Jones believes that it is impossible to run a business from outside the country. However it is possible to be an investor in the business with a native of the country functioning as an investor-manager.

Lastly, if you are just becoming familiar with franchising, international franchising will not interest you as an immediate opportunity. Owning, operating, and selling franchises in a foreign environment is not recommended for anyone who is not a seasoned franchisee or does not have considerable international business experience. All the things that can and do go wrong with any new business are multiplied when dealing with distance and different cultures and people.

The Ideal International Franchisee

The franchising relationship is often likened to a marriage. This comparison is heightened in the international franchise relationship, where a lengthy courting and engagement period normally precedes the ultimate "marriage." Some franchisors and franchisees are even asking for test-period arrangements, say, one or two years, before the final franchise agreement is signed.

The procedures can be painstaking because the stakes are big in international franchising. The franchise relationship, as we noted in the previous chapter, is usually that of a franchisor and a master franchisee. And the territory that is licensed to the master franchisee is not a zip code area or a portion of a state. Instead, the licensed area is quite often an entire country or a large portion of one.

Tip

The most attractive candidates for international franchises from the point of view of the franchisor are those who already own or lease good locations.

In general terms, these are the qualities and requirements the franchisor will be looking for in a master franchisee:

- The master franchisee should know the local market. This includes the culture, real estate opportunities, suppliers, financial institutions, and relevant laws and regulations.
- Ideally, the franchisee will have experience in the industry or business which is being franchised. In lieu of this, knowledge of and successful experience in a general business area is usually acceptable.
- Proven financial resources are a necessity. The master franchisee must have the wherewithal (either alone or most commonly with other investors) to buy the franchise rights, set up prototypes and systems, and develop the concept in the agreed upon territory.
- Proven management skills are another necessity. For the most part, the master franchisee will be functioning just as the franchise system does in its native country. That entails management skills in such areas as sales and marketing, training, and operations.
- The master franchisee should be enthusiastic and convinced about the feasibility of the franchisor's concept and system. Wanting to "do it your way" is a red flag to the franchisor.
- The franchisor looks for a certain "chemistry" in its master franchisee, which can be defined in part as integrity and a cooperative attitude.

Tip

If you have your sights set on a U.S. franchise—and you are a national of another country—the franchisor will require that you be able to communicate well in English.

Finding the International Franchise

If you are a national of the United States, Canada, or the United Kingdom, for example, and have an interest in a native franchise system for export to another country, you'll find the franchise the same way as you would for a domestic venture. You'll attend franchise shows, read the publications that list all the operating franchise systems, and talk to franchisees in your area.

Finding the right franchise when you are a native of, say, Hong Kong or Brazil and would like to operate a U.S. franchise in your country is a little more difficult. Here are some of the ways to locate the perfect franchise when operating from a distance:

- In foreign countries, the U.S. embassy offers a commercial service that helps local nationals learn about U.S. business opportunities. A "Gold Key" program offered by the embassy registers a foreign national and notes the specifics of the business interest (e.g., computer learning, printing) and the amount of the investment. The Commerce Desk then tries to match the prospective buyer with appropriate businesses. In the case of franchising, the franchisor will send high-level management to your country to discuss the opportunity.

- Contact a reputable franchise consultant who can set up meetings with viable and prescreened franchise systems which fit your qualifications. A fee is charged for this service, but it may save you much time and effort.

- Franchise expos are held in almost every major city in the world. This is a good way to survey the international franchise opportunities and follow up on the ones that interest you.

- The International Franchise Association (IFA) holds conferences in locations around the world where a variety of international franchise opportunities are presented by the principals of the company. These conferences are usually supported by major media advertising, such as in the Asian *Wall Street Journal* and the *International Herald Tribune.*

- Contact your local franchise association. Not every country has one, but most of the countries with strong franchising development have active associations. (See the Appendix for a listing of franchise associations.)

Forms of International Franchising

Although most franchise systems prefer a master franchise setup for their international expansion, other forms of agreements are sometimes chosen. These formats include the single-unit franchise, the area development agreement, or a joint venture agreement.

Master Franchise.   In this arrangement the master franchisee (also called the "subfranchisor") is granted a franchise for all or part of a target country. The master franchisee, which may be an individual, a group, or a company, has the right to develop the entire territory or subfranchise the units to a third party (subfranchisee).

The franchise system trains the master franchisee. In turn the master franchisee recruits and trains subfranchisees to operate individual units of the franchise. In effect, the master franchisee is now the franchisor in that country and receives a portion of the royalties for its support of individual franchises.

Area Development Franchise.   Similar to a master franchise agreement, a person, group, or company gains the right to develop an entire country or part of it. However, unlike the master franchise, the focus is on running the business, not selling franchises. The area developer does not receive the right to grant subfranchises. Substantial capital and management resources are necessary for the area developer, since there will be no subfranchisees to share the risks and capital requirements.

Single-Unit Franchise.   U.S. franchises rarely sanction a single unit outside the country with the possible exceptions of Canada and Mexico (because of their proximity). In this case a franchisee obtains the rights to open a unit of the franchise in his or her native country. Franchisors steer away from this type of arrangement because of the great costs sustained in servicing one unit outside the country.

Joint Ventures.   Two parties, the franchisor and the subfranchisor, make contributions to the investment in this arrangement. The parties negotiate their ownership shares and decide how to finance their contributions. Often the franchisors contribute expertise, a system, and sometimes cash. The foreign partners may contribute money and local knowledge. In essence, the joint venture company becomes the subfranchisor.

Franchise systems will usually not consider a joint venture arrangement, which puts their own capital at risk, unless the country is one they want to enter and they can't do it any other way. This is most common in Eastern European countries where the markets are promising but potential franchisees do not have the capital to totally fund the investment.

Checklist for Choosing an International Franchise Business

These are the basic questions you should be able to answer before getting down to serious negotiations with the franchisor.

Preliminary

1. Is there any regulation of foreign investments in your target country? Find out the details.

2. Are there any local laws and restrictions which would prohibit certain types of franchises?

3. Are there any import restrictions or laws governing the kinds of products or services which you can source from outside the country?

More Specific

4. Is there already an established demand for the franchise product or service? (It is very risky and expensive to try and create a demand where one does not already exist.)

5. Does the franchise have at least minimal name recognition? (The franchisor should have at least 25 outlets in a concentrated area.)

6. Is the franchise system financially strong and stable? (Companies looking for a quick buck will fail. The franchisor must commit to a longer pay-out period for international franchises.)

7. Is the system and the mindset of the franchise management flexible? (Often a part of the system has to be changed for a foreign market.)

8. Does the business have unique features that will give it an edge over the competition?

9. Are suppliers of the components, ingredients, equipment, or other needs of the business readily available?

10. Is the franchise trademark registered and protected in the target country?

Tip

Trademark protection is crucial for success. However, a franchise company frequently finds that its trademark has already been filed by someone else in the foreign country. This occurs because prior use is not a prerequisite for registration in many countries, unlike in the United States.

Japan is an example of a difficult market in which to register a trademark. An illustration occurred in the 1970s when a lawyer for McDonald's attempted to register the company's famous "golden arches" trademark. He found that a Japanese food distributor had registered the trademark just one day earlier. McDonald's finally obtained the right to use the golden arches, but the ownership of the trademark is still in doubt.

And so it is essential that you determine that the trademark is protected in your target country. Not only is this a prerequisite for you to do business, but also if the franchise company has to buy back a trademark from "pirates," the franchisee may be asked to pay part of the buy-back amount.

Contract Provisions

The details of the contract will vary with the type of agreement which is reached, i.e., master franchise, single unit, area development and joint venture. As you can imagine, a joint venture agreement can get very lengthy and complicated, since responsibilities and obligations for the two parties must be carefully spelled out. Engaging a competent franchise attorney is an absolute necessity in a joint venture agreement as well as any of the other international franchise formats.

Since the vast majority of international franchise agreements are master franchise setups, that is our focus. We will concentrate on the singular elements of an international agreement, and you should refer to Chapter 4 for the basics which remain the same for domestic or international agreements.

Initial Master Franchise Fees

Initial licensing fees are very often a source of conflict for the franchisor and the master franchisee. The challenge is to negotiate a fee, generally ranging from a low of $50,000 to over $1 million, which will reconcile the interests of the two parties.

The franchisor will probably insist on a substantial initial fee for all or some of the following reasons:

- The franchisor will be giving up the right to open up outlets or grant the franchises to a third party. The system wants compensation for the lost development opportunity.

- The international agreement will be costly to the franchisor in terms of financial and human resources. Some of the costs incurred are initial training of the subfranchisor and representatives, travel and living expenses for company executives sent to train and assist subfranchisors in the target country and possible replacements for these executives in the home country, and the registration of trademarks, translation of documents and sales materials, and assorted legal fees.

- The franchisor believes that a substantial fee will ensure that the subfranchisor is committed to the success of the franchise system in the target country.

The perspective of the subfranchisor is, of course, different. It will want to pay the smallest initial fee possible for the following reasons:

- The subfranchisor will assume the greater financial risk. Apart from the initial franchise fee, the subfranchisor will also have the following expenses: opening up a number of franchise outlets before enlisting subfranchises; establishing a training facility for subfranchisees; acquiring land and buildings or leasing the premises with a long-term liability; paying for the training, transportation, lodging, and meals of senior executives in the franchisor's country.

- The subfranchisor is exposed to significant business risk, since the franchise system is untested in the target country. In addition, the name recognition of the product or service may be nonexistent in the country.

- Depending on negotiations, the cost of the market research, translations of materials, and other similar obligations may be assumed in whole or in part by the subfranchisor.

Development Schedule

The rate at which franchise outlets will open is also an area of conflict for the franchisor and international subfranchisor. It is in the franchisor's interest to demand an aggressive development schedule, whereas the subfranchisor will want a conservative one. Expect prolonged negotiations before coming to an agreement on this question.

The franchisor feels justified in requiring that the subfranchisor open up the largest number of outlets in the smallest amount of time, since the company is giving up its development rights in the target country. Development of the market is controlled by the subfranchisor.

The subfranchisor, however, will not want to increase its financial and business risk by agreeing to an aggressive development schedule. An additional concern is that franchise outlets will be opened in secondary locations in order to keep up with the schedule, increasing the likelihood of the failure of the entire business.

Using a Test Period Agreement

One of the ways to help reconcile the opposing viewpoints of franchisor and subfranchisor is to enter into a test period agreement. The subfranchisor is granted the right and license in the exclusive territory with the obligation to open up a specific number of franchise outlets within a specific period of time. But the master franchise agreement is only entered into if the results of the test period are positive. The initial fee is not paid until a master franchise agreement is signed.

Test Period Agreement

If a test period agreement is utilized, other issues will have to be addressed. For example, who decides whether the master franchise agreement will be instituted? The franchisor or the subfranchisor can decide to go ahead or the decision can be mutual. (Negotiate for the right to make the decision!) Alternatively, the decision could depend on previously agreed upon criteria—such as outlets opened, sales volume achieved—which if met commit both parties to the execution of the master franchise agreement.

Since there is no master franchise agreement during the test period, the subfranchisor will usually enter into a unit franchise agreement for each unit opened. The standard unit agreement which is used in the home country can be utilized with, probably, a few adaptations. Some of these are the voiding of a payment of the initial unit fee (the initial master fee will be paid when the master franchise agreement is concluded), reduced royalty payments or none at all, and a different level of franchisor service.

The level and cost of training and assistance by the franchisor are issues that must be negotiated. Usually the franchisor will provide initial training which includes preopening, opening, and postopening assistance free of charge. Travel and hotel expenses associated with the training are sometimes paid by the subfranchisor.

The franchisor will usually require that the subfranchisor maintain strict confidentiality on proprietary information and know-how which is given to the subfranchisor during the test period. In the event that the master franchise agreement is not signed, the subfranchisor may be required to agree to not carry on a competing business.

The test period term is generally for a period of one or two years. The subfranchisor should allow sufficient time to make a reasonable assessment of the viability of the franchise system in the target country. Negotiate for more time if you think you need it.

The master franchise agreement will in all probability cover an entire country. For the test period the subfranchisor should limit the territory to a small region or a city.

Decide who will be in charge of advertising and promotion in the country during the test period. With a master franchise agreement, usually the subfranchisor is in charge of these areas.

Tip

Negotiate all the provisions of the master franchise agreement and attach it to the test period agreement so there are no surprises when the test period ends.

Outcome of the Test Period

If there is a decision not to proceed with the master franchise agreement, a few matters will have to be dealt with. One of these is the ownership of data and knowledge. It is customary that all such knowledge and know-how remain the exclusive property of the franchisor, but in special instances the parties may agree to a joint ownership.

Then there's the question of what to do with the franchise outlets which have been opened. Various possibilities may be considered. Often the unit franchise agreements are terminated and the outlets are liquidated with no trace of the franchise business remaining. This can be extremely costly for the subfranchisor, especially when land and buildings have been purchased and leasehold improvements made. Negotiate the cost of liquidation with the franchisor in the test period agreement and at least try for shared costs.

Another alternative is for the subfranchisor to operate the franchise outlets under the terms of each unit franchise agreement. No further expansion would be necessary, and a master franchise agreement would not be signed. If the subfranchisor decides not to operate the outlets, the agreement might allow the franchisor to buy the outlets on the basis of a predetermined price or formula. The franchisor might then develop the territory itself or grant a master franchise to a third party.

If the test period is positive, the parties will enter into a master franchise agreement. At this point the subfranchisor is required to pay the initial master franchise fee. On the positive side, the subfranchisor has tested the system and has reduced the risk to a minimum amount. From the point of view of the franchisor, however, a resulting positive test period can justify a substantial initial fee and require an aggressive development schedule.

Tip

All factors considered, my advice is to negotiate a test period agreement for any and all franchise businesses before finalizing a master franchise agreement.

Insights from a Banking Officer

Financing your international franchise investment, just like a domestic one, will be a challenge. And since we're talking in terms of developing an entire country market, the numbers will be much larger and the time spent in putting together the financial package will be considerable. Usually, a consortium or a group of individuals invest in a master franchise or area development agreement. It is rare that an individual will be able to finance and develop an international investment alone.

Tip

Most franchisors are not interested in individuals who put together an international deal using other people's money and contribute nothing themselves. Franchisors want successful entrepreneurs who will put their own money on the line.

In addition to the financial sources discussed earlier, some of the international banking institutions have developed franchising investment departments as an integral part of their business. One of these is The Royal Bank of Scotland and another is the Generale De Banque (Generale Bank) in Brussels, Belgium.

The franchising officer in the Brussels bank is Fons Durinck. His job is to assist any European who is interested in the financing of a franchise business. Generale Bank contends that it will try to finance international franchise agreements whenever possible. Durinck believes that a joint venture agreement works best. From the bank's point of view the franchisor is committing funds to the business, thereby increasing the chances for success. Although the bank will assist in master franchise financing, according to Durinck, it is considered risky in comparison to a joint venture with the franchisor's financial involvement.

From his exiences, Durinck has two bits of advice for would-be international franchisees. One, the banks are most impressed with franchisees who are very aware of the working conditions and social mores of the target country. Take the local culture of the country into account when preparing the franchise business plan. Second, be sure that the trademark of the system is accurately and legally registered before getting close to signing an agreement.

Trap

Beware. All successful franchise ideas don't transfer, and it's not always so easy to pick the winners. Consider this experience in Belgium: Kentucky Fried Chicken didn't work well in Belgium, and the natives didn't even want to try the frozen yogurt franchise products, but Chi-Chi's, a full-service Mexican restaurant franchise, is doing great!

An American in Hungary

George Hemingway is the managing director of Hemingway Holding AG, a public company which operates a variety of international businesses, some of which are franchises. Hemingway started out by buying companies in Hungary, businesses as diverse as gourmet shops and agricultural publishing. In the last few years, the company has concluded master franchise agreements for Hungary with Dunkin Donuts, KFC, and Pizza Hut franchise systems.

Hemingway says he saw an opportunity and acted on it. The McDonald's franchise was opening in Hungary, but no others seemed imminent, so he started talking to franchise systems which he thought would work in the country. Hemingway, though, wasn't starting cold. His company was already operating businesses there, so he was familiar with the culture, working habits, and problems of doing business in a former Soviet-bloc country. In fact, Hemingway, a resident of California with an office in Los Angeles, found it a necessity to spend over 50 percent of his time in Hungary to oversee the businesses.

The financing for the franchises was put together in the United States. The Hungarian government, says Hemingway, didn't give any financial help, although Hemingway could have obtained loans with very high rates. Hungarian nationals, however, are eligible for lower-rate enterprise loans.

Hemingway and his group negotiated obligations and performance objectives with each of the franchise systems. The company plans to subfranchise to Hungarian nationals and is already in the process of setting up local training centers for the sub-franchisees.

Adapting the franchises for the Hungarian population wasn't too difficult in spite of the cultural differences. The food and preparation of it stayed pretty much the same. A three-month supply of food was sent from the United States for the franchise unit's opening, but the company plans to eventually have 100 percent of the food supply produced in Hungary.

Hemingway did find that the decor and interiors of the franchise units had to be upgraded. An upscale look was necessary because the prices in the outlets are higher than Hungarian-owned food outlets. A fancier decor was a way to justify paying more, and it seemed to be something the local population craved. Hemingway gave local artists the job of decorating the outside and inside of the buildings, complete with murals. Most certainly, the Pizza Hut in Budapest with its elaborate Hollywood-style decor is a resounding success, and the lines of customers often stretch out onto the street. The other franchise units will continue the upscale image.

One big key to the group's success is their acquisition of prime real estate locations prior to negotiating the franchise agreements. The company, Hemingway states, still has good locations in its inventory for further site development.

Final Words

Experienced entrepreneurs will find international franchising a challenging and rewarding opportunity. The risks are greater than for domestic ventures but the payoff with a successful operation can be substantial.

11
Forewarned Is Forearmed: Common First-Year Problems

The business is like being on a train track.
Stop and the train runs over you.
                                        GEORGE COLGATE
                              V R Business Brokers franchisee

Starting up your new franchise business and taking it through the first year is an incredibly exciting time, not to mention tiring and often harrowing. When we asked a variety of franchisees in all parts of the United States what the major problems were in the first year of business, we naturally got a multitude of answers. But as we analyzed the answers carefully we realized that six answers came up more often than others.

Six Stumbling Blocks

Here are the problems most encountered by franchisees in the first year of operating a business, beginning with the most common one:

1. *Sales problems.*   Franchisees were challenged most by the sales end of the business, which brings with it "the need for constant sales pitches" and "cold calls." Selling requires the ability to close, to "get someone to make a decision to buy." They talked about the aftermath where they had to handle the "rejection and anxiety involved with making sales." Although some businesses require that more time be devoted to sales and others less, *every* business will require selling of some sort. There is no escape. So, if you cannot envision yourself in sales of any kind, even in small doses, you are probably not well-suited to operating a business.

2. *Getting good employees.*   With the unemployment rate hovering around the 7 percent mark, one would think that finding, hiring, and keeping good employees wouldn't be so difficult. Yet, those businesses that rely heavily on minimum-wage workers find that this is a sizeable problem for them. One way to reduce turnover in lower-paying jobs is to offer small increases on hourly wages for periods of employment, every three months, perhaps, or for increased productivity. It also helps if the owner establishes a personal rapport with the employees. (This goes for all employees, not just minimum-wage ones.) But perhaps the best advice is just to be realistic, since, as one franchisee told me, "no employee is ever as committed to the business as the owner."

3. *Undercapitalization.*   Securely in third place is "not having enough capital." Perhaps the build-out takes longer and costs more than expected, or maybe too much inventory is bought or no additional capital is allotted for slow payers—these are just a few of the things that can impact your capital situation. The best way to avoid this is to go through the suggested financial exercises in Chapter 4 with an eagle eye on the bottom-line figures. If you find there's a good possibility that your financial package will not get you through the first year, you essentially have two choices. One, you can go back to your financial sources and try to raise more capital *before* you buy the franchise, or, two, you can choose a new franchise which allows you to do business with the capital available.

4. *Sales shortfall.*   "Not reaching the projected sales figure" is the next problem area. Assuming the projected sales figures are reasonable for the business, the franchisee must sit down and analyze all

aspects of the business and pinpoint the weak link. This is a good time to call upon the franchisor's management and analytical skills in identifying anything which could be causing sales to fall short of realistic expectations.

5. *Delayed cash receipts.* The fifth-most-mentioned problem is "late payers." Unfortunately, delayed payment happens in almost all businesses that extend credit. You can alleviate this problem if you set up a system for payments from day one. Follow up immediately if a customer does not pay by the required date, and refuse credit terms to those deemed risky. The danger of having slow payers, of course, is that you will have difficulties meeting your own payments, such as monthly royalties and supplier bills. You might also evaluate whether you can convert your business to a pure cash basis from cash and credit.

6. *Time management.* "Managing priorities and operations" is the next cited problem. Running a business means you must priortize tasks. Most beginning franchisees find they have too many things to do and not enough time to do all of them. This feeling of panic usually disappears when the business grows enough so that the franchisee can hire employees to share some of the tasks. So too for managing the operational part of the business. Inexperience is usually the culprit here, and hard work and time usually solves the problem.

Problems with the System

Setbacks do occur, and businesses don't always progress the way we'd like them to. Usually, complaining and blaming the system won't help the problem. But sometimes you've done everything you can, and it looks like the problem lies with the system. Here are some steps you can take:

1. Contact the franchise system management. Do it both verbally and, more importantly, in writing. Pinpoint and explain the problem. For example, we can't keep customers because the products arrive late or the marketing and advertising material is unusable. Give as much solid documentation of the problem as you can.

2. Inform the franchise advisory council of your problem. If your problem is not remedied after contacting the franchisor, send a copy of the original letter explaining your problem to the advisory council. Follow up by phone and ask if the council has a plan of action. If your system doesn't have an advisory council, maybe now is the time to organize one with the other franchisees.

3. If the system infraction is serious, consult your attorney. See if there is a pattern with other franchisees as well. If so, ask them to document their cases.

4. As a very last resort, take your case to court and sue the franchise system. This course is not recommended unless the system's transgression is so blatant that nothing but the most extreme action will do. However, in most cases the franchise system will have deeper pockets and can outlast you in the prolonged period it takes the court to settle such a case, so try other methods first.

Our Informal Franchisee Survey

We conducted more than 50 interviews with current franchisees to gain the candid appraisals shared in this book. In my opinion, a textbook recitation of franchise opportunities and problems cannot compare with the honest evaluations of those "in the trenches."

The franchisees were chosen at random, from a variety of industries. About half of the franchisees were interviewed in person on their premises, and the other half by telephone. Here are the vital statistics on franchisees interviewed which I think, in many ways, represents a microcosm of franchising today.

Types of Businesses.   The types of industries represented are: retail food, business services, children's products and services, restaurants, weight control, communications, fast food, printing, residential cleaning, commercial cleaning, automotive, health and beauty, house/decorative products and services, package/mailing and shipping, photography, direct mail advertising, personnel services, security, retail stores, dry clean/laundry, signs, publishing, rental dresses, and check cashing.

Financing.   We looked at how franchisees financed their ventures. Many franchisees used combinations of financial sources, so numbers don't add up to 100 percent.

Personal savings	58%
Bank	24
System financing	12
Family/other investor	12
Government program	8
Note to seller	6
Line of credit	6
Home equity loan	4
General, limited partnership	2
Venture capital firm	2

Franchise Stage.   We investigated the stage of development of the franchise at purchase:

Start-up	26%
Early stages	38
Middle stages	30
Well developed	6

Ownership Period.   The time the franchise had been owned was established:

Under 1 year	15.0%
1 year	7.5
1 year plus	7.5
2 years	25.0
3 to 5 years	15.0
5 to 10 years	25.0
Over 10 years	5.0

Franchise Fees.   We investigated how much franchisees had paid in franchise fees:

Under $5000	2%
$5000 to $10,000	4

$10,000 to $20,000	45
$20,000 to $30,000	27
Over $30,000	14
Varies by region or territory	8

Royalty Fees.   When we asked about royalty fees, we got the following results:

No fee	8%
Up to 3 percent of gross sales	4
4 percent of gross sales	4
5 percent of gross sales	28
6 percent of gross sales	20
7 percent of gross sales	4
8 percent of gross sales	2
9 percent of gross sales	4
10 percent of gross sales	8
Above 10 percent of gross sales	8
Variable royalty on gross sales (0 to 15 percent)	14

Franchise Format.   Some franchise formats, such as multiple-unit ownership, are becoming more popular. We found these results with our polled franchisees.

Multiple-unit owners	34%
Resale owners	10
Conversions	4
Home-based businesses	24

General Satisfaction with Franchise.   Franchisees expressed the following rates of satisfaction:

Totally unsatisfied	2%
Somewhat unsatisfied	12
Satisfied	18
Very satisfied	16
Totally satisfied	52

The participants of our survey were as follows (several franchisees wished to be anonymous):

Kitty Alaily, Cost Cutters, City Looks, Wisconsin

Fred Banty, Padgett Business Services, Connecticut

Steve Bashein, AlphaGraphics, Washington, D.C.

Ann Brown, Computertots, Washington, D.C., and Maryland

Lisa Brumm, Formals Etc., Illinois

Mike Bueti, Merry Maids, New York

Ray Chappell and Paula Ford, Dent Doctor, Texas

George Colgate, VR Business Brokers, Tennessee

Carla Cunningham, Jani-King, Pennsylvania

Mary Cunningham, Decorating Den, Maryland

Camille DiNapoli, Subway, New York

Ken Dykhuis, Mighty Distributing Co., Illinois

Jeanette Fuller, Tutor Time, Florida

Larry Gambino, Priority Management, Inc., New York

Judy Gedman, FastSigns, New Mexico

Jim Gendreau, Cost Cutters, Minnesota

Leslie Goldberg, Expressions Custom Furniture, New York

Jeff Grayson, Pizzeria Uno, Florida

Arny Grushkin, Unishippers, Connecticut

Rich Habel, Mail Boxes, Etc., Washington, D.C.

Florence and George Hayden, Wendy's, Pennsylvania

Jeff Knight, GNC, New York

Danny Kostick, Pizza Hut, Pennsylvania

George Lawson, Red Hot & Blue, South Carolina

Nancy Mann, Citizens Against Crime, Georgia

Joan Maruyama, A Choice Nanny, Virginia

Robert Marziano, Aloette Cosmetics, New Jersey

Patrick McClune, Pressed 4 Time, New Jersey

Jay McDuffie, Check Express, Alabama

Linda Moore, Ledger Plus, Massachusetts

Eleanor Nesbit, A Choice Nanny, Florida

Tom Orban, I Can't Believe It's Yogurt, Pennsylvania, Virginia, Washington, D.C., Maryland

Barry Pasarew, Voice-tel, Texas

Rick Petersen, Interim Healthcare, New Hampshire

Carolyn Peterson, Headshots, New York

Marcy Pinnell, Wee-bag-it, Missouri

Barry Roberts, Execu-Train, New Jersey

Stuart and Sharon Ruben, Money Mailer, Connecticut and New York

Lisa Rutledge, Kinderdance Intl., North Carolina

Steve Saffar, The Wedding Pages, New Jersey, New York

Harold Sanchez, GNC, Connecticut

Glenn and Connie Schenenga, Future Kids, New York

Tom Swarm, Motophoto, Washington D.C., Maryland

Sharon Taylor, Potions & Lotions, New Mexico

Grace Thompson, Leadership Management Inc., Pennsylvania

Sandi Vettle, Leadership Management Inc., Pennsylvania

Ken Wisotzky, Gloria Jean's Coffee Bean, My Favorite Muffin, New Jersey

Larger-Survey Statistics

Some additional statistics indicating the attitudes and opinions of franchise owners are shown in the following list of major findings of a larger franchise survey and Figures 11-1a to 11-1g. These selected results are drawn from a market research study which was done in November and December 1991 by the Gallup Organization for the

International Franchise Association. Gallup interviewed, by telephone, a national sample of 994 franchise owners across the United
States:

1. Ninety-four percent of the respondents said that overall, they considered their franchise operation to be either very (47 percent) or
   somewhat (47 percent) successful.

2. Over 70 percent of the franchise owners said that their franchise
   operation had either exceeded or met their expectations with regard to both their personal satisfaction in operating the franchise
   (76 percent) and their overall satisfaction (73 percent).

3. More than 80 percent of the owners said their franchises had met
   most of or exceeded their expectations with regard to the number of hours they had to work (they had to work more). Also, the
   higher the owners' level of active involvement on a day-to-day basis with the franchise, the higher their level of satisfaction.

4. Seventy-five percent of the franchisees said that, if given the same
   opportunity (knowing what they know now), they would purchase
   or invest in the same franchise business again. Respondents who
   had income of $50,000 or more were more likely to reinvest (81
   percent).

5. Sixty-three percent of the owners were more satisfied with their
   franchise than with previous business experiences, and 23 percent reported the same level of satisfaction.

6. Seventy-nine percent rated their relationship with their franchise
   system as either excellent (39 percent) or good (40 percent); 6
   percent reported poor working relationships.

Comparison to Other Businesses/Jobs
Level of Overall Satisfaction as an Owner of a Franchise
Compared to Other Businesses Owned/Operated or Jobs Held
(n=994)

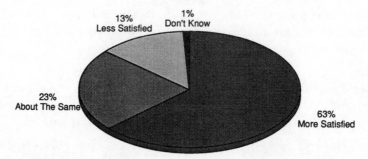

- Relative to other businesses they have owned or operated, or other jobs they have held, a majority of respondents (63%) reported they were more satisfied with the franchise operation. Only slightly more than one-tenth (13%) of the respondents said that previous businesses they had owned or operated or jobs they had held proved to be more satisfying than their current position of owning a franchise.

Figure 11-1*a*. Source: International Franchise Association.

American Workers/Franchise Owners

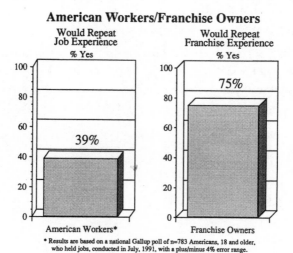

Figure 11-1*b*. Source: International Franchise Association.

Expectations
Level of Expectations Being Met for Various Aspects of the Franchise

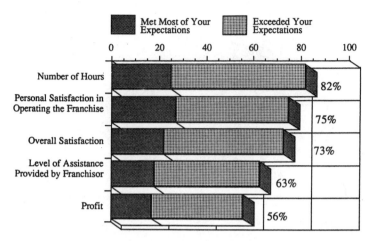

Figure 11-1c. Source: International Franchise Association.

Given Another Chance...
"Knowing what you know now, if given the opportunity,
would you purchase or invest in this same franchise business again?"
(n=994)

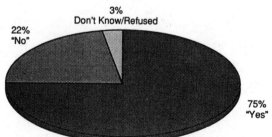

- Those respondents who tended to be most likely to repeat their franchise investment included:
  - respondents with annual gross incomes of $50,000 or more (81%)
  - respondents who own two or more franchises (79%)
  - respondents who had been in the business five years or less (77%)

Figure 11-1d. Source: International Franchise Association.

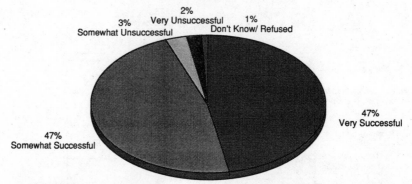

Overall Success

"Overall, would you consider your franchise operation to be
very successful, somewhat successful, somewhat unsuccessful or very unsuccessful?"
(n=994)

Almost all (94%) of the respondents said that overall, they considered their franchise operation to be either very (47%) or somewhat (47%) successful. Only one in fifty (2%) said they considered their franchise operation to be very unsuccessful.

Those respondents who tended to rate their franchise operation overall as being more successful included:
- respondents with incomes of $150,000 or more (67%)
- respondents who had been in business for 11 years or more (57%)

Figure 11-1e. Source: International Franchise Association.

Estimated Annual Gross Income Before Taxes
(n=994)

Response	% Total
Less than $50,000	26%
$50,000 to less than $100,000	23%
$100,000 to less than $300,000	26%
$300,000 or more	11%
Don't Know	2%
Refused	12%

• On average, respondents reported their annual gross income, before taxes, as a franchise owner was $124,290. Approximately one-half of the respondents (48%) reported a gross income under $100,000, while slightly more than one-third (36%) grossed over $100,000.

Figure 11-1f. Source: International Franchise Association.

Estimated Total Investment Cost
Including Franchise Fees and any Additional Expenses
(n=994)

Response	%Total
$50,000 or less	37%
$50,001 to $100,000	19%
$100,001 to $300,000	15%
$300,001 or more	11%
Don't Know	4%
Refused	14%
Mean Cost	**$147,570**

- As would be expected, respondents reported a wide variety of amounts of total investment cost that they incurred for their franchise. On average, however, respondents reported investing $147,570.

Figure 11-1g. Source: International Franchise Association.

Selected Contacts for Franchise Information

General Contact Organization

International Franchise
 Association
1350 New York Avenue, N.W.,
 Suite 900
Washington, DC 20005
(202) 628-8000
(202) 628-0812 (Fax)
Contact: William B. Cherkasky,
 president; Terrian Barnes-Bryant,
 vice president of Research,
 Minority and Women's Affairs

International Franchise Association Organization Members (Source: International Franchise Association)

Argentine Franchise Association
Santa Fe 995, piso 4, Buenos Aires
 1059 Argentina
(54) 1-3935263/393-5263 (Fax)
Contact: Mr. Oswaldo Marzorati,
 president

Franchisors Associations of
 Australia and New Zealand
Unit 9, 2-6 Hunter Street,
 Parramatta, NSW 2150 Australia
(61) 2-891 4933/2-891 4474 (Fax)
Contact: Mr. Bryce Bell, executive
 director

Austrian Franchising Association
Parkring 2, Vienna 1010 Austria
(43) 222-5128587/668-825671
(Fax)
Contact: Ms. Waltraud
Frauenhuber

Brazil Franchise Association
Travessa Meruipe, 18 Villa
Mariana, Sao Paulo 04012 Brazil
(55) 11-5711303/11-5755590 (Fax)
Contact: Mr. Bernard Jeger,
president

British Franchise Association
Thames View, Newtown Road
Henley on Thames, Oxon RG9
1HG England
(44) 491-578049/491-573517 (Fax)
Contact: Mr. Brian Smart, director

Canadian Franchise Association
5045 Orbitor Drive, Suite 201,
Bldg. 12,
Mississauga, ON L4W 4Y4, Canada
(416) 625-2896/(416) 625-9076
(Fax)
Contact: Mr. Richard B.
Cunningham, president

Danish Franchise Association
Amaliegade 37, Copenhagen 1256
Denmark
(45) 33-156011/33-910346
Contact: Mr. Peter Arendorff,
president

European Franchise Federation
9 Boulevard des Italiens, Pris
75002 France
(33) 1-42601452/1-42600311 (Fax)
Contact: Mr. Michael Micmacher,
chairman

Finnish Franchising Association
PL 212, Helsinki 0012 Finland
(358) 12-34584/12-34542 (Fax)
Contact: Mr. Antti Wathen,
chairman

French Franchise Federation
9 Boulevard des Italiens, Paris
75002 France
(33) 1-42600022/1-42600311 (Fax)
Contact: Ms. Chantal
Zimmer-Helou, president

German Franchise Association
Paul Heyse Str. 33-35, Munchen 2
8000 Germany
(49) 89-535027/89-531323 (Fax)
Contact: Mr. Hans Lang, director

Norway
Handelen Hovedorganisasjon
Postboks 2483, Solli, Oslo 2 0202
Norway
(47) 2-558220/2-558225 (Fax)
Contact: Mr. Per Reidarson,
president

Hong Kong Franchise Association
22/F Unit A United Centre, 95
Queensway, Hong Kong
(852) 529-9229/527-9843 (Fax)
Contact: Ms. Charlotte Chow,
manager

Hungarian Franchise Association
Secretariat: c/o Dasy, P.O. Box
446, Budapest H-153 Hungary
(36) 1-115-4619/1-135-9349 (Fax)
Contact: Dr. Istvan Kiss, secretary
general

Indonesia Franchise Association
Jl. Pembangunan 1/7, Jakarta
  10130 Indonesia
(62) 21-3800233/21-3802443 (Fax)
Contact: Mr. Arang Sukandar

Irish Franchise Association
13 Frankfield Terrace,
  Summerhill, South Cork, Ireland
(353) 21-270859
Contact: Mr. John Neenan,
  director

Italian Franchise Association
Corso di Porta Nuova, 3, Milano
  20121 Italy
(39) 2-29003779/2-6555919
Contact: Pier Luigi Pitto, chairman

Japan Franchise Association
Elsa Bldg. 602, Roppongi, 3-13-12,
  Minato-ku Tokyo 106 Japan
(81) 3-34010421/3-34232019
Contact: Mr. Haruyasu Orihashi,
  executive managing director

Mexican Franchise Association
Insurgentes Sur 1783, #303, Col.
  Guadalupe Inn,
Mexico, DF 01020
(52) 5-524-8043/5-524-8043 (Fax)
Contact: Mr. Adolfo Crespo,
  director general

Netherlands Franchise Association
Boomberglaan 12, Hilversum
  1217 RR the Netherlands
(31) 35-243444/35-249194 (Fax)
Contact: Mr. Ton Vervoort,
  chairman

Associacao Portuguesa Da
  Franchise
Rua Castilho, 14, Lisboa 1200
  Portugal
(351) 1-574778/1-542220 (Fax)
Contact: Ms. Pascale Lagneaux,
  director general

South African Franchise
  Association
Kenlaw House, 27 De Beer Street,
  P.O. Box 31708,
Braamfontein 2017, South Africa
(27) 11-4033468/11-4031279 (Fax)
Contact: Mr. Jack Barber,
  executive director

Swedish Franchise Association
Box 55112, Stockholm 114 8
  Sweden
(46) 8-6608610/8-6627457
Contact: Mr. Stig Sohlberg, chief
  executive officer

Swiss Franchise Association
Seefeldrain 5 Luzern 6006
  Switzerland
(41) 41-328870/41-328860 (Fax)
Contact: Mr. Marc Bernard Frei,
  president

Franchise Show Schedules

Blenheim Franchise Shows
1133 Louisiana Avenue, #210
Winter Park, FL 32789
(407) 647-8521

Franchise Consultants and Site Selection

Franchise Business USA
7423 Courthouse Road,
  Spotsylvania, Virginia 225583
(703) 582-9500; (703) 582-9225
  (Fax)
Contact: Carl Carlsson

Lending Sources

Allied Lending Corp. (subsidiary
  of Allied Capital Corp.)
1666 K Street, N.W., Suite 901
Washington, DC 20006
(202) 331-1112

AT&T Commercial Finance Corp.
5613 DTC Parkway, Suite 450
Englewood, CO 80111
(303) 741-4144

AT&T Small Business Lending
  Corporation
44 Whippany Road
Morristown, NJ 07962
(201) 397-3000

Bank of Montreal
Commercial Banking
  Headquarters
First Canadian Place, 18th floor
Toronto, Ontario
CANADA M5X 1A1
(416) 867-5234

The Bank of Nova Scotia
  (Scotiabank)
44 King St. West
Toronto, Ontario
CANADA M5H 1H1
(416) 866-4377

Bay Bank and Trust Company
509 Harrison
Panama City, FL 32401
(904) 769-3333

Business Loan Center, Inc.
704 Broadway, 2nd floor
New York, NY 10003
(212) 979-6688

Canadian Imperial Bank of
  Commerce
Commerce Court Postal Station
Toronto, Ontario
CANADA M5L 1A2
(416) 784-6825

Capital Funding Services
P.O. Box 424
Waco, TX 76703
(817) 753-3114

CAPTEC Financial Group, Inc.
315 E. Eisenhower Parkway, Suite 315
Ann Arbor, MI 48108
(313) 994-5505

Chrysler First Business Credit Corp.
24 Olivia Drive
Yardley, PA 19067
(215) 321-3305

Diamond Capital Corporation
805 Third Avenue, Suite 1100
New York, NY 10022
(212) 838-1255

First Western SBLC, Inc.
18301 Biscayne Blvd.
2d floor–South
North Miami Beach, FL 33160
(305) 933-5858; (800) 969-3223

Franchise Capital Corporation
1935 Camino Vida Roble
Carlsbad, CA 92008-6599
(619) 431-9100; (800) 421-7188

Generale De Banque
Montagne du Parc 3
Brussels, Belgium 1000
Tel: 32.2.516.4091; Fax: 32.2.516.4543
Contact: Mr. Fons Durinck

Gulf American, Inc.
P.O. Box 191
Panama City, FL 32405
(904) 769-3200; (800) 228-9868

Independence Mortgage, Inc.
3010 LBJ Freeway, Suite 920
Dallas, TX 75234
(214) 247-1776

ITT Small Business Finance Corporation
2055 Craigshire Road, Suite 400
St. Louis, MO 63146
(314) 576-0872; (800) 447-2025

Kanaly Trust Company
4550 Post Oak Place, Suite 139
Houston, TX 77027
(713) 626-9483

LoanSource Financial Services
700 E. Park Blvd.
Suite 102
Plano, TX 75074
(800) 962-6912

Melrose Financial Network
Intracoastal 3000 Bldg.
3000 N.E. 30th Place
Suite 208
Ft. Lauderdale, FL 33306
(305) 566-9770; (305) 566-0770 (Fax)

The Money Store Investment Corporation
17530 Ventura Blvd.
Encino, CA 91316
(818) 906-2999; (800) 362-3071

National Cooperative Bank
1630 Connecticut Avenue, N.W.
Washington, DC 20009
(202) 745-4691

National Westminster Bank PLC.
4th floor, National House
14 Moorgate
London, UK EC2R 6BS
(011) 44-71-726-1666

National Westminster Bank USA
592 Fifth Avenue
New York, NY 10036
(212) 602-2842

Pacific Funding Group
17534 Von Karman Avenue
Irvine, CA 92714
(714) 474-1788

Phoenix Leasing Incorporated
2401 Kerner Blvd.
San Rafael, CA 94901
(415) 485-4840

PMC Capital, Inc.
17290 Preston Rd.
Dallas, TX 75252
(214) 380-0044; (800) 486-3223;
 (214) 380-1371 (Fax)

Royal Bank of Canada
Head Office, 1, Place Ville-Marie
Montreal, Quebec
CANADA H3C 3A9
(514) 874-3102

The Royal Bank of Scotland
Franchise and Licensing
 Department
42 St. Andrew Square
Edinburgh EH22YE Scotland
Tel: 031-523 2178; Fax: 031-229
 2416

SANWA Business Credit
 Corporation
One South Wacker Drive, Suite
 3900
Chicago, IL 60606
(800) 331-5247

Southwestern Commercial
 Capital, Inc.
1336 E. Court Street
Sequin, TX 78155
(512) 379-0380

Stephens Franchise Finance
1400 Worthen Bank Building
Little Rock, AR 72201
(501) 374-6036; (800) 234-2271

Federal Government Small Business Sources

General:

Office of External Affairs
U.S. Small Business
 Administration
409 3d St., SW Room 7177
Washington, DC 20416
(202) 205-6607; (202) 205-7064
 (Fax)

*SBA regional offices (source of
certified and preferred lenders in
your area):*

*Region 1 (Massachusetts, Connecti-
cut, Maine, New Hampshire, Rhode
Island, Vermont):*

60 Batterymarch St.
Boston, MA 02110
(617) 223-2023

Region 2 (New Jersey, New York, Puerto Rico):

26 Federal Plaza, Room 29-118
New York, NY 10278
(212) 264-7772

Region 3 (Delaware, District of Columbia, Maryland, Pennsylvania, Virginia, West Virginia):

Allendale Square, Suite 201
475 Allendale Rd.
King of Prussia, PA 19406
(215) 962-3700; (215) 962-3800

Region 4 (Alabama, Florida, Georgia, Kentucky, Mississippi, North Carolina, South Carolina, Tennessee)

1375 Peachtree St., NE
Atlanta, GA 30367
(404) 347-2797

Region 5 (Illinois, Indiana, Michigan, Minnesota, Ohio, Wisconsin):

230 S. Dearborn St.
Room 510
Chicago, IL 60604

Region 6 (Arkansas, Lousiana, New Mexico, Oklahoma, Texas):

8625 King George Drive, Bldg. C
Dallas, TX 75235
(214) 767-7643

Region 7 (Iowa, Kansas, Missouri, Nebraska):

911 Walnut St., 13th floor
Kansas City, MO 64106
(816) 374-3605

Region 8 (Colorado, Montana, North Dakato, South Dakota, Utah, Wyoming):

One Denver Place–North Tower
999 18th St., Suite 701
Denver, CO 80202
(303) 294-7149

Region 9 (Arizona, California, Hawaii, Nevada):

Federal Bldg, Room 15307
450 Golden Gate Avenue
San Francisco, CA 94102
(415) 556-7487

Region 10 (Alaska, Idaho, Oregon, Washington):

2615 4th Avenue, Room 440
Seattle, WA 98121
(206) 442-7646

For a directory of operating Small Business Investment Companies and Minority Enterprise Small Business Investment Companies:

Mr. John Edson
Investment Division
Small Business Administration
1441 L Street, NW, Room 810
Washington, DC 20416
(202) 653-2806

Business Development Resources for Minorities and Women

U.S. Department of Commerce,
Minority Business Development
Agency (MBDA)
Room 5096
14th and Constitution Avenue,
NW
Washington, DC 20230
Contact: Janice Dessaso (202)
482-3261

The MBDA regional or district offices are broken into regions:

Atlanta region (Alabama, Florida, Georgia, Kentucky, Mississippi, North Carolina, South Carolina, Tennessee):

Carlton Eccles
MBDA Regional Director
401 W. Peachtree St., N.W.
Suite 1930
Atlanta, GA 30308-3516
(404) 730-3300

Rodolfo Suarez
MBDA Miami District Officer
51 S.W. First Ave.
Room 1314, Box 25
Miami, FL 33130
(305) 536-5054

Chicago region (Illinois, Indiana, Iowa, Kansas, Michigan, Minnesota, Missouri, Nebraska, Ohio, Wisconsin):

David Vega
MBDA Regional Director
55 E. Monroe St., Suite 1440
Chicago, IL 60603
(312) 353-0182

Dallas region (Arkansas, Colorado, Louisiana, Montana, New Mexico, North Dakota, Oklahoma, South Dakota, Texas, Utah, Wyoming):

Melda Cabrera
MBDA Regional Director
1100 Commerce St., Room 7823
Dallas, TX 75242
(214) 767-8001

New York region (Connecticut, Maine, Massachusetts, New Hampshire, New Jersey, New York, Puerto Rico, Rhode Island, Vermont, Virgin Islands):

John Iglehart
MBDA Regional Director
26 Federal Plaza, Room 3720
New York, NY 10278
(212) 264-3262

Shelley Schwartz
MBDA Boston District Officer
10 Causeway St., Room 418
Boston, MA 02222-1041
(617) 565-6850

San Francisco region (Alaska, American Samoa, Arizona, California, Hawaii, Idaho, Nevada, Oregon, Washington):

Xavier Mena
MBDA Regional Director
221 Main St., Room 1280
San Francisco, CA 94105
(415) 744-3001

Rodolfo Guerra
MBDA Los Angeles District Officer
977 North Broadway, Suite 201
Los Angeles, CA 90012
(213) 894-7157

Washington region (Delaware, Maryland, Pennsylvania, Virginia, Washington, D.C., West Virginia):

Georgina Sanchez
MBDA Regional Director
1255 22d St. NW, Ste.701
Washington, DC 20036
(202) 467-0012

Alfonso Jackson
MBDA Philadelphia District
  Officer
600 Arch St., Room 10128
Philadelphia, PA 19106
(215) 597-9236

Financial and Technical Assistance

Association of Small Business
Development Centers
1313 Farnam on the Mall, Suite
  132
Omaha, NE 68182-0472
(404) 595-2387

Business Assistance Consortium,
  Inc.
Franchise Financing Program
6600 N.W., 27th Avenue
Miami, FL 33147
(305) 693-3550

The Combined Fund, Inc.
915 E. Hyde Park Boulevard
Chicago, IL 60615
(312) 363-0300

Department of Commerce
  Minority
Business Development Agency
Office of Program Development
14th & Constitution, Room #5096
Washington, DC 20230
(202) 482-3261

Franchise Resource Assistance
Training Program
Howard University School of
  Business and Public
  Administration
Small Business Development Center
Room 128
Washington, DC 20059
(202) 806-1550

Jacksonville Franchise Development
Program Economic Development
  Company
128 E. Forsyth Street, Suite 500
Jacksonville, FL 32202
(904) 630-1914

Miami-Dade Franchise Technical
Assistance Center of the Chamber
  of Commerce
6600 NW 27th Avenue
Miami, FL 33147
(305) 693-3550

New York State Minority and
  Women
Revolving Loan Fund of the
  Urban Development Corporation
1515 Broadway
New York, NY 10036
(212) 930-0452

Shingler-Hollis Investment Group,
  Inc.
1384 E Street, N.E.
Washington, DC 20002
(202) 397-1326

The Maryland Small Business
  Development
Financing Authority Equity
  Participation
Investment Program
217 E. Redwood Street, Suite 2240
Baltimore, MD 21202
(410) 333-4270

Pennsylvania Department of
  Commerce
Minority Business Development
  Authority
Forum Bldg., Room 404
Harrisburg, PA 17120
(717) 783-1128

Midwest Development
  Corporation
Franchise Development Project
P.O. Box 29405
Cincinnati, OH 45229
(513) 281-7814

Minority Business Organizations

American Indian Trade and
  Development Council
2 Union Square
601 Union Street, #430
Seattle, WA 98101
(206) 224-4338

Asia-Pacific American Chamber of
  Commerce
1112 Carper Street
McLean, VA 22101
(703) 893-4088

Association of American Indian
  Affairs
245 5th Avenue, Suite 1801
New York, NY 10016
(212) 689-8720

Institute for American Business
1275 K Street, N.W., Room 601
Washington, DC 20005
(202) 408-5418

League of United Latin American
  Citizens
900 E. Karen, Suite C-215
Las Vegas, NV 89109
(702) 737-1240

National Association for the
  Advancement of Colored People
  (NAACP)
Economic Development Office
604 Central Avenue
East Orange, NJ 07018
(201) 672-0211

National Black MBA Association
180 N. Michigan, Suite 1820
Chicago, IL 60601
(312) 236-2622

National Business League
1629 K Street N.W., Suite 605
Washington, DC 20006
(202) 466-5483

National Indian American
  Chamber of Commerce
1155 Connecticut Avenue, N.W.,
  #500
Washington, DC 20036
(202) 429-6588

National Minority Business
  Council
235 E. 42d Street
New York, NY 10017
(212) 573-2385

National Urban League
500 E. 62d Street
New York, NY 10021
(212) 310-9000

National Council of LaRaza
20 F Street, N.W., 2d floor
Washington, DC 20001
(202) 289-1380

National Minority Supplier
  Development Council
15 W. 39th Street, 9th floor
New York, NY 10018
(212) 944-2430

U.S. Pan Asian American
  Chamber of Commerce
1625 K St. N.W., Suite 380
Washington, DC 20006
(202) 638-1764

U.S. Hispanic Chamber of
  Commerce
1030 15th Street, N.W., Suite 206
Washington, DC 20005
(202) 842-1212

Women's Groups

American Business Women's
  Association
9100 Ward Parkway
P.O. Box 8728
Kansas City, MO 64114
(816) 361-6621

American Woman's Economic
  Development Corporation
71 Vanderbilt Ave.
New York, NY 10169
(212) 692-9100

National Association of Black
  Women Entrepreneurs
P.O. Box 1375
Detroit, MI 48231
(313) 341-7400

National Association for Female
  Executives
127 West 24th Street
New York, NY 10011
(212) 645-0770

National Association of Negro
  Business and Professional
  Women's Club
1806 New Hampshire Avenue, N.W.
Washington, DC 20009
(202) 483-4206

National Association of Women
  Business Owners
600 S. Federal Street, Suite 400
Chicago, IL 60605
(312) 346-2330

National Council of Negro Women
1667 K Street, N.W., Suite 700
Washington, DC 20036
(202) 659-0006

Veterans

VetFran
1010 N. University Parks Drive
P.O. Box 3146
Waco, TX 76707
(817) 753-4555; (817) 756-7757
  (Fax)

Index